Every Closed Eye Ain't Sleep

African American Perspectives on the Achievement Gap

Teresa D. Hill

ROWMAN & LITTLEFIELD EDUCATION

A division of

ROWMAN & LITTLEFIELD PUBLISHERS, INC.

Lanham • New York • Toronto • Plymouth, UK

Published by Rowman & Littlefield Education
A division of Rowman & Littlefield Publishers, Inc.
A wholly owned subsidiary of The Rowman & Littlefield Publishing Group, Inc.
4501 Forbes Boulevard, Suite 200, Lanham, Maryland 20706
http://www.rowmaneducation.com

Estover Road, Plymouth PL6 7PY, United Kingdom

British Library Cataloguing in Publication Information Available

Library of Congress Cataloging-in-Publication Data

Hill, Teresa D.
 Every closed eye ain't sleep : African American perspectives on the achievement gap / Teresa D. Hill.
 p. cm.
 Includes bibliographical references.
 ISBN 978-1-61048-104-5 (cloth : alk. paper)—ISBN 978-1-61048-105-2 (pbk. : alk. paper)—ISBN 978-1-61048-106-9 (electronic)
 1. African Americans—Education. 2. Academic achievement—United States.
 3. African American students—Social conditions. I. Title.
 LC2717.H55 2011
 371.829'96073—dc22

2011012951

♾ ™ The paper used in this publication meets the minimum requirements of American National Standard for Information Sciences—Permanence of Paper for Printed Library Materials, ANSI/NISO Z39.48-1992.

Printed in the United States of America

For Willa—potential . . . gone too soon
For David—hope . . . worth the struggle
For countless generations of beautiful, intelligent, strong children
who hold in their eyes visions of the future,
and
For those who've gone before. . . .

Contents

Prologue

A Vision

"Where there is no vision, the people perish. . . ." (Prov. 29:18)

On a summer day just before the start of school, a 17-year-old African American boy played Russian Roulette with a few of his friends. He loaded the gun and, without spinning the chamber, pointed it to his head. "Now you see me, now you don't," were his last words as he pulled the trigger. He died instantly.

Day after day, we encounter anonymous casualties in our fight against self-destruction. The people in the community where I came of age handle the fight in the same way as most others: they either take cover, or they risk their lives to join the fight. Some die fighting for the living, some die trying to kill, some live in the trenches, and some make their escape. "War is hell," they say.

As you enter the city, you are greeted by a sign that says, "Welcome . . . Population 35,800." After spending some time here, you know the sign is false. The population is ever increasing, mostly due to new births. The city is around 80 percent Black and Hispanic. Ethnic Europeans make up a small percentage, and the White Americans that complete the picture are the left-overs of the "White flight" that has taken place over the last twenty years.

Entering the city, you lock your doors, not out of paranoia but out of "common sense." There is a high crime rate here. Periodically, people will visit you with new appliances for "bargain" prices. As a longtime citizen, you know what to buy and what to let go. You know what paths to take, and you know not to walk alone at night. You are familiar with the sound of gun shots. It has become almost instinctive for you to take cover when a gun sounds.

Almost all of the children you know are Black. They attend all Black schools. Most of them are very smart; they can learn almost anything, but they don't. The schools don't really focus on educating them. You know that most of them will receive a mediocre education, if they receive one at all. The kids are "street smart." You know, they know their way around the world compared to other kids. They are used to being under authority, so they either submit to it or rebel completely. The rebels are often victims of the streets. You struggle to keep your kids safe by teaching them to be strong and independent. You teach them to respect authority and themselves. Each of them is important to you and you train them well for the coming battles.

Every morning, you get up and go to work like most of the other citizens of the city. Your job pays pretty well. You care for your children and work hard to see that they have the things they need and want. However, like most of your neighbors, you know several people on welfare (including the working poor, the unemployed poor, and the willing poor). You've seen children roaming the streets at all times of the night. You've seen women and children beaten. You've lost quite a few friends and acquaintances to the streets. Yet you've also seen children do well in school, win awards, grow up, get educations, become successful, and get married. You've celebrated the birth of children, only to later mourn their loss.

The world that you know is filled with every kind of pain, every kind of passion, every kind of hatred, every kind of joy, and every kind of love. You try, everyday, to balance the contradictions because, if you don't, you will surely go insane. Everything you know and love is in the city. You've been away, but it is always with you. The images never leave, and of all the battlefields in the world, your tour of duty is here.

There are cities and towns like this one throughout the country. This work arose out of a vision for people like me, who have called them home. I believe we can save our children from being casualties in the war against racism, violence, educational deprivation, and self-destruction. And we can provide all of our children with the quality of education that will give them choices in life.

MY SOUL LOOKS BACK AND WONDERS . . .

I recognize that who I am and the experiences that I have had are factors in my work. What follows is my attempt to describe the experiences that drove me to act on these beliefs.

In 1991, I sat as a student in Mr. Mackenzie's junior-level honors U.S. History class. One of Mr. Mackenzie's tasks, as was the case with all junior-level history teachers, was to prepare us for the U.S. Constitution test. Mr. Mackenzie was thorough. He taught us about all aspects of the Constitution. He taught us how our government was founded and how it was meant to work together. He taught us about the balance of power and how the Constitution was structured to be a "living document."

Mr. Mackenzie taught us about the Bill of Rights and the freedoms that are guaranteed to citizens. He taught us how the Constitution stemmed from other documents like the Magna Carta and the Declaration of Independence. Mr. Mackenzie spoke about the democratic beliefs of all men being created equal and the right to "life, liberty and the pursuit of happiness." He engaged us in conversations about our history, our ideals, and about what it meant to be an American. He did everything that a history teacher is supposed to do.

Then, with the turn of a phrase, Mr. Mackenzie changed my life. In the fall of 1991, he uttered the words "Three-Fifths Compromise." The Three-Fifths Compromise (Article 1, Section 2, Paragraph 3 of the United States Constitution) defined slaves as three-fifths of a person for purposes of taxation and representation. The poignancy of this lies in the fact that these Africans were not defined based on their rights or standing as individuals. They were not defined in terms of their origins or potential. In the document that framed our government and nation, our nation defined Blacks strictly as objects for the purpose of securing the economic and political standing of White men.

The argument over whether Black slaves would be counted as a person had nothing to do with whether Blacks were human beings. The question of whether slaves would count as people was not about the slaves at all. It was a compromise arising out of a negotiation. What's more, our Constitution defined Africans, not in response to questions about their status in the United States, but in response to the economic and political needs and whims of Whites.

Human beings have a right to self-determination and a need to define themselves instead of being defined by others. And yet, in our nation, African Americans, Blacks, "negroes," "coloreds," "niggers," etc., were defined by others for the purposes of economic and political power. This realization brought down the ideals that seemed so noble.

The scary realization struck me that in this country that I loved, "liberty and justice for all" did not and had never existed. Thomas Jefferson's assertion that "all men are created equal" did not apply to people like me. The Constitution that later guaranteed "equal protection under the law" had made a specific exception for people like me. Suddenly, it all became clear in my 16-year-old mind that all of it was just talk.

That year I looked at my high school, where I had received what I thought and still believe to be an outstanding education with all the things that I needed; with numerous opportunities; with teachers who knew me and trusted me and whom I trusted; with a cohort of students that I liked and got to know very well; with opportunities laid out in front of me and with high expectations. I looked at other students, and I noticed that the outstanding education that I was receiving was not available to others. It was clear to me as I looked around that the path that had been laid out for me had been blocked off for others.

I lived a dual existence. In high school, I was perched perilously between the two opinions of my peer groups. With my Black peers I was referred to as "talking proper" and "like the Whites." When with my White peers, it was observed that I was not like other Blacks. "You're just like us" one of my White friends observed as we sat in economics class, "You're not like the others." (I later came to know this as "honorary Whiteness.")

I received the education I had not because I deserved it above others, but because I was chosen. Early in my schooling, some White person, and many White people and a few Black ones after that, looked at me and decided that I could be something special and then acted upon that belief. They spent extra time with me, placed me in "gifted" classes, recommended me for community programs, talked with me about a variety of careers, gave me lots of awards and recognition, selected me for leadership positions, and gave me the benefit of the doubt. That "sponsored mobility" benefited me greatly.

What haunted me was that there were so many others who would never have what I had. I could not understand why we would not give every child the quality of education I received. My research is colored by my experiences as a student, teacher candidate, school administrator, district administrator, and mother in predominantly White school systems serving children from different backgrounds. I became an educator and school administrator with one purpose in mind. My quest is that every school day, every class, every lesson would be a form of sponsored mobility, and that every child would have the options and opportunities that history has so often closed off. I write as a practitioner and a parent.

If my mission is for every child, why does this work focus on African American children? Simply put, this work focuses on Black children because Black children need the support. I submit that, in this country, just by virtue of being born Black, an African American child is less likely to survive infancy, less likely to receive a quality and complete education, more likely to be poor, more likely to lose friends or family members to violence, and guaranteed to face the horrors of personal and institutional racism.

I hope this work will prompt researchers, policymakers, and educators to start a dialogue about educating African American children on different terms, to address the achievement gap as an issue of social justice, and to operate under the belief that all children can learn . . . period.

T. D. H.

Introduction

Every Closed Eye Ain't Sleep

Daddy used to say, "Every closed eye ain't sleep; every goodbye ain't gone." His reminder warned us not to make assumptions. This advice has served me well many times through the years, particularly as an educator of low-income and African American children. The commonly held belief is that students struggle behaviorally and fail academically in school because their parents don't care or because they are part of a culture that devalues education. However, experience working with African American children and parents teaches that the apparently "closed eyes" of parents when it comes to schools should not be taken as an indication that parents are "asleep" when it comes to education. The African American community has a reputation of being asleep to ensuring the well-being of its children. It is time to challenge that assumption.

Contrary to popular belief, throughout history, education has held high status among African Americans. The belief that education is the way to improve one's life continues to be taught within the African American community. Given this fact, it is disconcerting to see the lagging achievement of many schools that serve large numbers of African American children. Despite the cultural belief that education is the way to climb the social and economic ladder, and despite the promotion of education to children from within the community, statistics show that African American children are outperformed by White students in almost every measure of educational achievement and attainment.

The results of the National Assessment of Educational Progress (NAEP 2007) report that the average African American eighth-grade student performs at the same level as the average White fourth grader. There is a 29 point gap between the average score of White students and the average

1

score of African American students in grades 8 and 11. In addition, the National Educational Longitudinal Study (NELS), which has been used in numerous educational studies, documents that educational attainment of African Americans lags behind that of Whites, although improvements have been made over the last 30 years.

The achievement gap represents a contradiction. One might expect that if a group of people believes in education, that belief in and commitment to education will be reflected in the achievement of its students. However, this has not been the case with African American students. The African American community has a unique relationship with the American educational system. This relationship is a strained one at best because, although African American people believe in and are committed to education, they overwhelmingly do not trust the education system to operate in the best interests of African American children. There is a disconnection between what the African American community believes about education and what the African American community experiences in schools.

Clearly, there are structures that hinder schools from meeting the needs of all students, and there are structures that hinder African American children from achieving success in school. Schools were not designed to produce high levels of success for all students. Promoting creativity and critical thinking among all students was not their goal, nor was giving all students a high level of skill in reading, writing, and mathematics. In fact, Industrial Age common schools were designed for the express purpose of socialization and sorting. It was their job, in a newly industrialized society, to provide workers with the level of skill necessary to do menial labor in factories.

Schools needed to socialize large numbers of children to be prompt, obedient workers. They were designed to identify and separate those students who were considered capable of becoming higher level workers and managers. For those students, it was necessary to provide a more liberal education that would prepare them for the level of leadership they would assume. Still other students attended elite schools. They were educated for creativity, competition, leadership, rhetorical skills, and higher order thinking.

When we expect public schools to educate all children to high levels, we are asking schools to do something they were never designed to do. It is erroneous to say that our schools are failing. Our schools are not failing; they are very successful at doing what they were designed to do. If we want schools to fulfill a new charge to educate all children to high levels, we must redesign schools for that new purpose.

In the old system of socialize and sort, it was clear that African American children were almost exclusively relegated to the kind of schools and classes that would prepare them to do what society designated as appropriate for an inferior race. They were trained to be obedient and subservient, to submit to authority without question, to do menial jobs of manual labor for minimal wages, and to never interfere with the rights and privileges of Whites. Siddle-Walker (2001) explains that many Southern schools for Black children actually broke out of this mold. Run by highly educated Black teachers and administrators, these schools provided a high-quality education for Black children within their own communities. However, this high quality of education was not supported when schools went through the process of desegregation.

When schools were integrated, Black children were removed from these learning environments and placed in the common schools, where they were subject to the training deemed appropriate for them. The education of African Americans in the common schools was designed to maintain oppression. There was no expectation that Blacks would do anything above their level of training. Author James Baldwin wrote of the limitation of African Americans:

> This innocent country set you down in a ghetto in which, in fact, it intended that you should perish . . . You were born where you were born and faced the future you faced because you were black and for no other reason. The limits of your ambition were, thus, expected to be set forever. You were born into a society which spelled out with brutal clarity, and in as many ways as possible, that you were a worthless human being. You were not expected to aspire to excellence. You were expected to make peace with mediocrity. (1976, p. 7)

As a part of their socialization, it was expected that students would understand that they had no part in the rights and privileges of Whites. Public schools were designed to ensure that the written and unwritten rules of race and class would be maintained throughout successive generations.

Now America faces an interesting dilemma. We are at a time in history in which many would rather forget that such limitations based on race and class existed. Unfortunately, because schools were designed to preserve the status quo, including inequality, it is impossible to erase these limitations without redesigning schools themselves. The No Child Left Behind Act was passed in 2000 with the statement that it was time for us to leave behind the "soft bigotry of low expectations" (George W. Bush 2000). The law created accountability measures to encourage schools to meet the needs of all children aiming at 100 percent proficiency by 2014. NCLB has made African American student achievement very important in the eyes of schools. However, the law does not raise the importance of the African American children as people; rather, it raises the importance of their test scores. This results in the use of a variety of means to raise the scores, sometimes planned with little or no regard to the needs of children.

The basis of this work is the insights gained from interviews designed to access the African American discourse on education. The things we say and the way we talk about events and ideas are the best evidence of our culture, what we believe, and the way we live. Discourse not only includes the things that we say in formal settings such as during speeches and in the media, but it also includes the things we talk about with our friends, the ways in which we interact with our spouses and families, the stories we tell our children, and the things we recall and share. This book examines this discourse. It is particularly important in studying the needs of African American children because the nature of the racial division in our nation has limited outsiders from accessing the personal and community discourse that takes place within the African American community. As a result, those that influence educational policies have little or no access to African American community members' ideas and beliefs about the education system.

In "standard" American English grammar, a subject is something or someone that acts while an object is someone or something that is acted upon. Past research has seldom focused on treating African Americans as the subject of the study. It is typical for studies to focus on statistics and other measures and discuss African Americans as those acted upon by outward factors instead of as actors with their own beliefs, choices, and expectations.

Traditional research has studied African Americans in opposition to Whites, identifying the ways in which African Americans differ from Whites. In this book, I make an effort to view African American community members' beliefs without Whiteness or "mainstream" culture as the lens. I will explore African American beliefs that relate to the achievement gap and demonstrate that the starting point for creating an education system that meets the needs of all children is learning about the children and the community that we serve. In this way, I will recognize African Americans as thinkers and actors. The foundation upon which a better education system must be built is the knowledge, beliefs, ideals, and experiences of the people our educational system serves.

This work traces the idea of the achievement gap through history, identifies the ways in which beliefs about African Americans have affected their schooling, examines African American community members' conceptual framework about education, and proposes the ways in which this generation can redesign schools. The starting point of this process is to open a dialogue with the people the schools must serve.

In Chapter 1, I focus on defining the achievement gap phenomenon and the discourse that supports it. I provide an operational definition of the achievement gap that will allow us to trace it through history. I also describe the current achievement gap discourse that supports the perpetuation of the gap. The chapter then maps the origins of the achievement gap and tracks its existence into modern times.

In Chapter 2, I go on to review the traditional research on the achievement gap and African American education. I discuss the findings of this research and the ways in which it has influenced the education of Black students. Chapter 3 describes the methodology used for accessing the African American discourse.

In Chapter 4, I present a conceptual framework based on the discourse shared by the research participants and explore the roles, responsibilities, and expectations inherent in what I have termed the "educational transaction." I also discuss the participants' analysis of the achievement gap in light of this framework. In Chapter 5, I expose the ideological conflicts that help to perpetuate the achievement gap. I juxtapose the educational transaction framework with the "mainstream" view of the educational process. I conclude by offering guidance for those who desire to improve education for African Americans.

The work is based on some basic assumptions. First, throughout this work, I will refer to racial groups and use the common racial terms "White," "Hispanic," "African American," and "Black." This should not be misconstrued as a validation of the idea of race as a biological reality. Biological races do not exist in human beings. Research shows that I, as a Black woman, have as much DNA in common with a White woman as with an African woman. In addition, the range of physical features among people who are considered to be Black is as wide as the range of physical features between Whites and Blacks (Graves 2005).

Race is a social construct that was created for social reasons and is maintained by social means. Although race is not a biological reality, it is a social, political, and economic reality that affects each of us as individuals and as members of groups. Because we operate in the social, political, and economic realm, race is real and race does matter. When a child is born, his/her race is listed on the birth certificate. He/she carries this designation throughout life. Our racial designation effects who we are, what we do, and to a greater or lesser extent, the choices we make, the opportunities we have, the way people interact with us, and the expectations that are placed before us. Although, I do not believe in race as a biological reality, I do believe that race is a reality of life in American society.

I will also repeatedly use the terms "liberal" and "conservative" to describe two contrasting ways of thinking about politics, economics, social realities, and public policy. These two ways of thinking do not represent a pure dichotomy. These beliefs, all of which are positive in their own way, lie along a continuum. The liberal end of the continuum focuses on the values of social responsibility, cooperation, and government intervention. The conservative end of the continuum focuses on personal responsibility, meritocracy, and small government. Neither of these approaches to democracy is "right" or "wrong." They have both participated in shaping our system of education and the achievement gap.

Throughout this work, I will discuss the history of education as it relates to African Americans. Part of that history is racism, discrimination, and the belief that African Americans are inferior. I will use the terms that were used in history. I will not edit quotations or otherwise modify information from its original form. I believe it is important that we do not sterilize our racial history. In sharing information from history, I am not endorsing the racist beliefs that were held. I am simply recognizing the effect these beliefs have had on our history. For example, the fact that I believe Herrnstein and Murray's *The Bell Curve* (1994) is a racist manifesto and that the authors are promoting the most vile and insidious kind of racism does not change the fact that *The Bell Curve* represents an important part of the history of the achievement gap.

I operate under the conviction that all people are created equal and "endowed by their creator with certain inalienable rights" one of which, I believe, is the fundamental right to an education. I make no arguments to justify my belief in human equality, and I will make no arguments to convince others of this basic truth. (The Bible advises that one should not argue with a fool.) All human beings are inherently equal. Race, class, and gender are not determinants of intelligence, character, or potential.

I recognize that the achievement gap is not solely an issue of race. Gaps in educational achievement affect many different ethnic groups as well as people from low-income backgrounds and those with disabilities. Each educational achievement gap is important and indicative of a larger problem that is caused by schools that were designed to sort students rather than ensure that all succeed. Studies of how the achievement gap is structured for any of these groups are warranted. However, the focus of this book is the gap as it relates to African Americans.

It is important to note that this book is not designed to be just another exploration of the test score gap. Numerous other books and articles provide a description of the difference in scores among various groups. This book is designed to help the reader understand that other perspectives on the achievement gap exist and that they impact the work that schools do with African American children. The perspectives that will be shared are based on a combination of history, research, personal anecdotes from African American community members, and personal experiences.

Although researchers are typically expected to write objectively and to separate themselves from the research analysis and conclusions, I make no attempt to write as an objective observer. The personal experiences, anecdotes, and beliefs of individuals are valid and meaningful, and they have a significant impact on the way groups of people see the world. In order for the reader to understand and/or appreciate this book, the reader must be able to consider the idea that others may see the world differently.

In order to create schools that truly exist to meet the educational needs of all children, we must design schools for that purpose. If we want to have schools in which African American children learn and are successful, we must design schools based on their needs. If we want our rhetoric about education to match our experience in schools, then we must come together and open a discourse about what African American children need. We must recognize that this is a conversation that has never before been held on equal terms.

Chapter 1

Tracing the Achievement Gap Discourse

Education has been used as a tool for both the oppression and the advancement of Black people. It was denied to prevent uprising, limited to insure dependence, segregated to deny equality, and biased to produce inferiority. Yet, throughout our history, African Americans have valued education almost as highly as freedom. While in the history of "mainstream" society, education has been used to teach citizens to make the most of freedom, among African Americans, education has been seen as a means to achieve it.

As Dr. Michael Ford, Dean of Multicultural Affairs at Hampshire College, asserted in 1991:

> There is an unbroken link between the newly freed slaves who fought for universal state-supported public schools in the South and the black mothers and fathers who from the 1950s through the 1980s sent their children in search of a better education on foot and in school buses into the teeth of hostile and sometimes violent white resistance. This determined battle for schooling has been fueled by a commitment to literacy and personal development not just as a means to enhance social mobility but as keys to inclusion in this society as full and equal citizens. (p. 748)

The importance of education is supported by the realization that the educational system possesses two important qualities. First, schooling, because of its status as a state-supported, state-sanctioned, and state-mandated institution, has the power to communicate the attitudes of the government and the greater society to the masses. Those that control education greatly influence the nation's attitudes about right and wrong, superior and inferior, good and bad.

Second, through the course of history, schooling has gained the distinction of being the institution in which children are prepared not just to function in

9

society, but, moreover, to function in a specific place in the society. Schooling presents a reality to students who eventually come to accept and perpetuate that reality. Carter G. Woodson (1933) argued that schooling solves the problem of controlling the oppressed. Education gives the oppressor control of the minds of the oppressed. Once the student's mind is controlled, his actions are controlled along with it.

> You do not have to tell him not to stand here. . . . He will find his "proper place" and will stay in it. You do not need to send him to the back door. He will go without being told. In fact, if there is not back door, he will cut one for his special benefit. His education makes it necessary. (1933, p. xiii)

This may seem trivial, but it raised an infinite number of questions. What is the purpose of education? Should schools emphasize classical education or vocational training? Should making a living be the only goal of education or do students need something more? W. E. B. Du Bois (1903) expounded on this question in *The Souls of Black Folk*, "Training for life teaches living; but what training for the profitable living together of black men and white? . . . To make here in human education the necessary combination of the permanent and the contingent—of the ideal and the practical in workable equilibrium—has been there, as it ever must be in every age and place, a matter of infinite experiment and frequent mistakes" (p. 77).

The value of education and the cultural belief that education is the key to social and educational advancement have persisted throughout the history of Africans in America despite the many obstacles to quality education for African Americans. The African American cultural discourse on education provides insight into the past, present, and future of African American education.

THE ACHIEVEMENT GAP DISCOURSE

Despite the belief in the value of education, African Americans continue to have fewer positive outcomes in public education beginning as early as kindergarten and continuing through all levels of education. African American students are more likely to be retained in grade, more likely to be placed in special education, more likely to receive suspensions and other severe disciplinary actions, less likely to take pre-college, honors, or AP level courses, less likely to graduate from high school, and less likely to enter and complete college than White students. This pattern is so pervasive in American education that the prominent mainstream discourse on the education of African Americans is framed in terms of underachievement.

African American students have been labeled as pathological, deprived, underprivileged, at-risk, urban, and most recently, diverse. The question of how to provide high-quality education for African Americans is framed in discussions of remediation, compensatory education, and at-risk programming. The fact that this is the prevalent discourse, despite the success of many African American individuals in the educational system, denotes the significance of the gap in outcomes between African Americans and Whites.

Standardized testing, heralded as the scientific way of measuring human intellectual ability and academic achievement, has permeated the fabric of American education. The tests, ranging from IQ tests and college entrance exams to kindergarten screening tests, are used widely to make decisions regarding individuals, groups, and entire educational systems. Standardized and intelligence tests support the predominant discourse of inequality by identifying a gap in scores between African Americans and Whites. This gap, quantified as 15 points or one standard deviation to the benefit of the latter, is evident across socioeconomic groups and persistent over time (Herrnstein & Murray 1994).

The use of norm-referenced testing is so accepted that educators have begun to trust the outcomes of such tests, incorporating the results into their belief system about the capabilities of different children. In fact, the gap in scores is so well documented that many educators have come to accept the difference in educational outcomes between Blacks and Whites to be inevitable. This is evident in the discourse on the education of African Americans and other "minorities." The gap in educational outcomes has been studied and described in various manners since the origin of our nation. Most recently, it has been termed the achievement gap.

Examples of the achievement gap discourse are numerous in the popular media. The recurring themes of the discourse are the intractability of the gap and explanations for the existence of the gap. Headlines explaining that Black student achievement lags behind that of White students and statements that the achievement gap between races persists can be found frequently in cities throughout the country. *The New York Times* reported that tests in reading and math showed that over a year's period, minority students and low-income students scored lower and grew less than White students and middle-class students (June 1, 2007). Both popular news media and periodicals aimed at educators contribute to the achievement gap discourse.

A May 2007 article in a Cleveland, Ohio newspaper exemplified the second theme of the discourse with the opening statement, "The achievement gap separating black boys from just about everyone else springs from a powerful, anti-education culture rising in the black community. . . ." (*Cleveland Plain Dealer,* May 16, 2007). Newspapers, journal articles, and books frequently explore perceived reasons for the underachievement of African American children.

The discourse surrounding the gap also permeates the education profession. The achievement gap discourse among educators involves perpetuating the idea that different groups of students can be expected to perform differently and that some groups of students are trouble. The achievement gap discourse often demonstrates the favored status of some groups over others. Educators sometimes refer to "the good parents" or describe a child's parents as "very involved" when advocating for preferential treatment.

Educators can sometimes be heard referring to "those kids" or "these kids" when referring to African American, Hispanic, or low-income children. Even well-meaning educators often protest that "these kids" cannot be expected to meet certain standards. They prefer to focus on "caring" for the students and making them feel comfortable.

I recall my experience as a first-year teacher in a high-poverty school serving African American children. The school used a reading/school reform model known as *Success For All*. The model required that students throughout the school be grouped for instruction based on their reading level. These groupings were made regardless of grade level. As a result, fourth grade students were expected to participate in reading groups with first and second grade students. This particular school only served students through fourth grade. At the fifth grade level, students moved to a middle school in the same district along with students from several other schools in the city. The middle school did not use *Success For All*.

Under the school's implementation of *Success For All*, a fourth grade student in a first grade reading group could receive an "A" in reading. On one occasion, I asked the staff member charged with training new staff on the use of *Success For All*, "What happens when a child finishes fourth grade and still reads at a first grade level?" Her response was, "Then we've given him four years of success." The school was so focused on providing a feeling of success, no plans were made to ensure that students developed the skills they needed.

The other key component of the achievement gap discourse involves the adage "All children can learn." When discussing school and school district vision and mission statements, the phrase "all children can learn" is often offered as the basis of educators' beliefs. Typically, however, educators go on to qualify that statement with a host of ifs, ands, buts, and other qualifiers. For example, "All children can learn [but only] at their ability level," "All children can learn [but only] to their potential," "All children can learn [but only] at their own pace," etc. Each of these statements allows the educator to determine the child's ability, pace, or potential.

THE ACHIEVEMENT GAP DEFINED

To fully explore the achievement gap and its effects on the education of African Americans in American society, it is necessary to have a working definition of the achievement gap. The term is used by educators to denote the failure and underachievement of students (typically those who are African American, Hispanic, and/or low-income) in comparison to the middle-class Whites of mainstream society. It is important to be clear that the term "achievement gap" can be defined as both a phenomenon and a social construct. This is where the achievement gap finds the power to perpetuate itself by replicating itself in successive generations.

The achievement gap phenomenon can be defined as the roughly one standard deviation difference in scores on standardized and/or norm-referenced tests and the quantifiable difference in grades and other educational outcomes that is evident between racial and social groups (particularly African Americans, Hispanics, Whites, and low-income and middle-class students) in the American educational system. This phenomenon is evidenced by measures such as intelligence test scores, college entrance exams, standardized achievement tests, graduation rates, college entrance rates, and college completion rates.

It is important to note that this is an actual phenomenon. Its existence is a matter of fact based on available statistics on educational performance. The phenomenon, that is, the fact that differences exist in educational outcomes, must be overcome. Tactics such as legal requirements (e.g., No Child Left Behind) and school reform models focus on the achievement gap phenomenon with little or attention to the social construct.

The achievement gap as a social construct is far more complex. The achievement gap as a social construct can be defined as the societal belief that the quantifiable differences in educational, social, and economic scores and outcomes of the different races and classes are based on "true"/"real," authentic differences in the intellectual ability, academic potential, social viability, and moral proclivity of different groups. It essentially posits that these differences (all to the benefit of members of the White middle class who are seen as the norm) are a matter of fact that governs the relationships among and the outcomes of diverse groups.

The social construct of the achievement gap is based in "Whiteness," a belief system in which the values, beliefs, behaviors, ideas, and characteristics of mainstream White middle-class society are the norm by which all other groups and individuals are to be measured and compared (hooks 1997). In this comparison, the attitudes, behaviors, beliefs, values, ideas, and characteristics of all others, especially African Americans in opposition to whom Whiteness was conceived and characterized, become abnormal, dysfunctional, patho-logical, depraved, oppositional, and inferior (hooks 1997).

In this way of thinking, then, children who demonstrate these behaviors in opposition to Whiteness in the school system are now identified with the euphemistic term "at-risk." Measures aimed at closing the achievement gap seldom address the social construct. In fact, in most cases these measures and strategies are steeped in the social construct of the achievement gap.

For the purposes of this book, the achievement gap phenomenon described previously will be referred to as the "outcome gap." The social construct that I have described will be referred to as the "achievement gap ideology." It is important to differentiate the phenomenon from the social construct because each warrants a different response and each must be eliminated in order for the achievement gap to disappear.

Both the outcome gap and the achievement gap ideology are critically important to the quest for the education of African American children. The outcome gap demonstrates that public education has not been successful in meeting the needs of African American students to the same level as Whites. It promotes the societal and school-based expectation of "underachievement" and it creates and perpetuates a cycle of low achievement as many educators and community members see the outcome gap as evidence low ability. In addition, the achievement gap ideology builds on the outcome gap to lend credence to the American belief in Black inferiority and provide rationale for social and economic injustice. The achievement gap ideology supports the assumption of "Whiteness" as the standard for which schools are designed and policies planned.

Combating the achievement gap and the mentalities it promotes should be at the forefront of leadership for social justice. It is the new front of the civil rights movement. The quest for quality education for African American children must be undertaken without preconceived notions because the needs of African American children cannot be meaningfully addressed through the lens of Whiteness.

The current fascination with researching the achievement gap is well-justified given its importance; however, the traditional scope and focus of the research serves to only support the perpetuation of the gap. In this book, I review the development of the achievement gap ideology, the history of African American educational thought in relation to the achievement gap ideology, traditional research that has shaped educators' approaches to edu-cating African American children, emerging alternatives to this research, and pedagogical approaches for African American success. I then share insights gained through interviews aimed at accessing the contemporary African American discourse on quality education.

ORIGINS OF THE ACHIEVEMENT GAP IDEOLOGY

The achievement gap ideology originated long before the development of the common school in the United States. In fact, it is older than the United States. The achievement gap ideology originated in the rationalization of slavery, the denial of rights to Black people, and the persecution of other groups.

The achievement gap ideology became prevalent through the advancement of Black inferiority theory. In 1776, Thomas Jefferson wrote the words "We hold these truths to be self evident, that all men are created equal. They are endowed by their Creator with certain unalienable rights, these being Life, Liberty and the Pursuit of Happiness" (Jefferson 1776, p. 14). In 1787, the same year in which the Constitution of the United States was ratified, Thomas Jefferson wrote *Notes on the State of Virginia*, in which he argued with the same fervor that Blacks had inferior reasoning faculties than White men (Jefferson 1787). His view was that:

> Comparing them by their faculties or memory, reason, and imagination, it appears to me, that in memory they are equal to the whites; in reason much inferior, as I think one could scarcely be found capable of tracing and comprehending the investigations of Euclid; and that in imagination they are dull, tasteless, and anomalous. . . . (Jefferson 1787, p. 15)

Regarding the education of Blacks, Jefferson noted that with all the advantages of being in the company of Whites, Blacks had never managed to demonstrate cultural development (Jefferson 1787). In response to anti-slavery activists, Jefferson argued,

> Many millions of them have been brought to, and born in America. Most of them indeed have been confined to tillage, to their own homes, and their own society: yet many have been so situated, they might have availed themselves of the conversation of their masters; many have been brought up to the handicraft arts, and from that circumstance have always been associated with the whites. Some have been liberally educated, and all have lived in countries where the arts and sciences are cultivated to a considerable degree, and have had before their eyes samples of the best works from abroad. . . . But never yet could I find that a black had uttered a thought above the level of plain narration; never see even an elementary trait of painting or sculpture. (Jefferson 1787, p. 15)

We will encounter this belief in the inherent advantage of being around Whites again later in the development of the achievement gap ideology.

In a famous ongoing debate about Benjamin Banneker, Jefferson espoused the achievement gap ideology (Jefferson 1787). The debate centered around the talents of Benjamin Banneker, who was being upheld by some as an example of what Blacks could accomplish. Jefferson, impressed with Banneker's apparent intelligence and skill, at first wavered from his almost instinctual belief in the inferiority of Blacks. Later, however, he stood firm on this point (Jordan 1969). Jefferson argued that although Banneker had accomplished much in comparison to other Blacks, he was an underachiever in comparison to Whites. He summed up his views by saying,

> Upon the whole, though we admit him to the first place among those of his own color who have presented themselves to the public judgment, yet when we compare him with the writers of the race among who he lived, and particularly with the epistolary class, in which he has taken his own stand, we are compelled to enroll him at the bottom of the column. (Jefferson 1787, p. 151)

The achievement gap ideology, the belief in the inherent inferiority of Blacks, was debated among the forefathers of the society. It was vital to the continuation of slavery in the United States.

Other theorists used a different approach to support the achievement gap ideology. Edward Long, a lawyer from Jamaica, sought a more scientific approach to the study of the Negro race, basing his ideas on his views of biology. He attributed the differences in the Negro—Black skin color that does not change, "a covering of wool, like the bestial fleece, instead of hair," large nose and lips, a "bestial or faetid smell, which they all have in a greater or lesser degree," complete lack of genius and morality, and barbarity—to genetic differences (Long 1788, p. 29).

It was his thought that Black people differed enough from humans to be classified as a variant species in the same genus. What is more, he related Blacks to the orangutan:

> [The orang-outan] (*sic*) has in form a much nearer resemblance to the Negro race, than the latter bear to white men; the supposition then is well founded, that the brain, and intellectual organs, so far as they are dependent upon mere matter, though similar in texture and modification to those of other men, may in some of the Negro race be so constituted as not to result in the same effects. (p. 32)

Biblical theologies of the creation of the races promoted that idea that the characteristics of the races were immutable and that the mistreatment of a cursed race was justified and morally right. Blacks were considered to be the children of Cain, the biblical son of Adam who was cursed for murdering his brother. Later, this idea was changed to cast Black people as the cursed children of Noah (Jordan 1969). Noah had three sons that became the progenitors of the entire human race after the flood. Ham, the youngest son, made the mistake of seeing his father naked and telling his brothers about it. As a result, when Noah was no longer inebriated, he cursed one of Ham's sons. "And he said, Cursed be Canaan; a servant of servants shall he be unto his brethren" (Genesis 9:25, KJV).

Canaan, they believed, was the father of all of the Blacks of Africa. This explained why Blacks would be condemned to slavery as a class. It also provided justification for a new kind of slavery. The same biblical passage goes onto describe the future generations of Noah's other two sons. It was postulated that from Shem's line would arise the Jews, Arabs, and Semitic peoples (Jordan 1969). Their blessings would come through their religious knowledge. Japheth's descendents would become the Europeans. Their blessing according to the passage would be a high level of knowledge and technological and other advancement. Japheth's descendents would be rulers. This biblical rationale for the existence of race and race-based oppression was used widely.

Theologians went on to use biblical passages about the duties of slaves as teachings to encourage slaves to willingly submit to their oppression. They promoted and sometimes even forced slaves to convert to Christianity, believing that it would cause the slaves to be well-behaved. It was also a part of a systematic process of stripping the former Africans of their identity.

The social institution of slavery advanced the achievement gap ideology. To rationalize slavery, slave holders promoted the belief that Blacks were less than human and that the best thing for Blacks was to be taken care of by White slave holders. Blacks were treated at worst like animals and at best like perpetual children. Slaves were only educated to do the menial tasks that were assigned to them and to learn parts of the Bible that were considered to support slavery. Even this rudimentary education of slaves was not advocated by all, however, as it was said that to educate the Negro was to make him unfit to assume his rightful and beneficial position as a slave (Katz 1967). The other problem with the education of slaves, argued opponents of the education of Blacks, was that it increased the danger of rebellion or escape.

By the time of the passage of the Fugitive Slave Act in 1792, the Southern states had begun to battle the education of slaves by passing laws against teaching slaves to read and write. These laws, strengthened after the infamous Nat Turner Rebellion of 1831, which struck fear in the hearts of slave owners, provided harsh punishment for teachers of slaves (Woodson 1922). Eventually, slaves were even forbidden to read the Bible. This prohibition against education was so strict that people could be thrown in jail or lynched for teaching slaves to read.

After the end of the Civil War, Southern White society was threatened by the rapid advancement of Blacks during the Reconstruction period. With the Reconstruction Era legislation regulating the opportunities of the newly freedmen, Blacks began to be educated in their own schools and churches. Clauses respecting the provision of public education for all were inserted into the new constitutions of the Southern states. With this assistance, the schools for Blacks grew in enrollment. By the end of the Reconstruction in 1877, the Black schools were serving a greater percentage of the Black children than the White schools were serving of White children. Also, the length of the school year in Black schools typically exceeded that of the White schools. Surprisingly, in some areas the Black teachers during this time were paid more than the White teachers (Tuzon 1993).

The Reconstruction Era brought about the establishment of colleges and universities for Blacks. Freedmen also assumed majority status in some local and state governments. These advancements were a threat to the achievement gap ideology. However, the ideology would quickly rebound with the help of a deal to end Reconstruction.

By the 1890s in Alabama, as in many other states, White citizens had begun to fight the advancement of education for Blacks with two major complaints:

> . . . first, that blacks in the black belt counties received nearly all of the area's school funds while paying virtually no taxes; and second, that black pupils were *not mentally advanced to the point where they needed as much education as white pupils* [italics added], and therefore did not need as much money for their education. (Tuzon 1993, p. 89)

Then, in 1891, the Alabama legislature passed a bill giving the superintendent of schools the authority to distribute funds to schools in a way that was "just and equitable" (Tuzon 1993, p. 88). This resulted in a dramatic decrease in funding for Black schools since it was not considered just for so much funding to be given to schools for the education of inferior people. The average income of Black teachers declined sharply from that point on. On the other hand, the length of the school year, enrollment, and average teacher income increased greatly during the same period of time (Tuzon 1993).

By the early 1900s, the advance of scientific inquiry and the rise of Darwinism and later social Darwinism supported the achievement gap ideology. Craniometry sought to explain the lack of ability of African American by measuring first the skulls and then the brain cavities of people of different races (Burnham 1985). First, researchers measured the skulls of Whites and Blacks hoping to relate skull size to intelligence. However, they found that the skulls of Blacks on average were larger than those of Whites. Next, they began to measure the brain cavities and weigh the brains of cadavers believing that this would show that Whites had larger, and therefore more intelligent, brains.

Charles Darwin's theory of evolution was used in a manner similar to the biblical stories of Cain and Noah to explain the origins of the races. The theory of races included three races that were said to include all people (Burnham 1985). The races were known as Caucasoid, Mongoloid, and Negroid. The Caucasoid race included White Europeans and Arabs. The Mongoloid race consisted of Asians. The Negroid race included Blacks from Africa. Black inferiority theorists decided that humans developed into different races based on the evolutionary needs of the habitats in which they lived. Blacks, then, were the least evolved for a variety of reasons including the harshness of the environment in which they lived.

This theory argued that Blacks had never evolved beyond the level of hunters and gatherers. They never had to learn agriculture. They never made cultural advancements. They were essentially un-evolved. In this way of thinking, Europeans became the most highly evolved race. Early in the development of humanity, the group that would become Caucasians traveled north to settle. There they faced the challenge of having to survive in a colder climate. They had to adapt to the intellectual demands of building an agricultural community. This caused Caucasians to developed more high-level intellectual and moral skills (Jordan 1969). The idea that Blacks were inherently inferior due to the process of evolution would reappear later in a much more persistent form.

Sociologists and political scientists began to apply Darwin's premise of survival of the fittest to the study of the world's socio-political systems. The central belief of social Darwinism is that those who are strong will survive and succeed and the weak will flounder and die out. The death of the weak is inevitable, expected, and acceptable. Applying this theory, supporting the weak is ineffectual for the individual and damaging for the society. Human beings must evolve socially through a process similar to natural selection.

Blacks, it was argued, had to evolve socially and culturally before they would be ready to bear the responsibility of liberal education and political power (Tuzon 1993). If Black people failed to evolve socially, it was reasonable that they would remain as a social, political, and economic underclass. Social Darwinism remains as a powerful premise of the achievement gap ideology.

The development of the standardized tests was the next major step in the devel-opment of the achievement gap ideology. The IQ test, developed in France by Alfred Binet, was first used by the U.S. Army in 1905 (Miller 1974). Although the test was designed to determine which school children might need additional academic help, the test was used as a mechanism to sort individuals based on their ability to serve in different roles. When applied to African Americans, testing clearly demonstrated that African Americans had less intelligence and aptitude as measured by the tests than Whites of various social standings. By

1915, standardized tests were being used for college admittance decisions. The era of testing was just beginning. Norm-referenced tests would continue to play a significant role in educational opportunities of African Americans.

Binet's test was developed at the beginning of the eugenics movement. It was believed that one could identify those genes that were most desirable and engineer the advancement of those genes. The most desirable genes were those that included White skin. This movement continued in prominence for several years but then declined when Adolf Hitler began to use the "science" of eugenics to justify his genocide (Miller 1974). Still, the results of this movement have never disappeared.

The measurement of the outcome gap through norm-referenced tests began during the era in which Black inferiority was the prevailing belief. The standardized test is firmly rooted in the achievement gap ideology. Intelligence tests were designed to differentiate groups and individuals from one another and to efficiently identify those individuals who possessed the desired characteristics and those who did not. Throughout the history of these tests, they have demonstrated that African American do not possess the characteristics desired by mainstream White society.

One extremely important result of the rise of standardized tests is the popular acceptance idea of the normal curve. The normal curve is essentially a statistical construct. However, it takes on new meaning when applied as a support for the achievement gap ideology. The normal curve is used to support the sorting of people by standardized test scores. It assumes that "normal" is a given score and that half of the population will score at or above the normal score and half will score below normal. The power of the idea of normal curve lies in the fact that it is expected that many people will fail. Others will succeed and educators have little power to influence this. This is especially the case when one takes into account that intelligence is seen as fixed at a relatively young age.

The achievement gap ideology is part of the fabric of American society. The idea that the differences in outcomes among different groups are due to authentic differences in the ability and worth of different races existed at the origin of the common schools. It continues to have a major influence on African American education. The key ideas of the achievement gap ideology recur throughout the years of research on African American education. We will see the inherent inferiority of Blacks, comparison judgments of Blacks, Darwinism and social Darwinism, norm-referenced tests and the normal curve reappear in multiple forms in research about African American education. Next, we will consider how some of these ideas influenced African American educational thought.

African American Educational Thought

There are two views of the Negro question. One is that the Negro should stoop to conquer; that he should accept in silence the denial of his political rights, that he should not brave the displeasure of white men by protesting. . . . There are others who believe that the Negro owes this nation no apology for his presence . . . ; that being black he is not less a man; that he should refuse to be assigned an inferior place by his fellow countrymen. (Meier 1963, p. 59)

From the beginning of the debate about educating African American children, African American leaders combated the achievement gap ideology. Frederick Douglass told the story of his own quest to learn how to read. Taking advantage of the poverty of a White child, Douglass persuaded the child to teach him how to read. The young Douglass paid the child with bread on the condition that the child would teach Douglass everything he learned in school (Douglass 1845). Douglass went on to escape from slavery and become a well-known abolitionist.

In his advocacy for the end of slavery, Douglass challenged the achievement gap ideology. He conceded that Blacks were inferior to Whites in that Whites could do what Blacks had never been allowed to do.

But while I make this admission, I utterly deny, that we are originally, or naturally, or practically, or in any way, or in any important sense, inferior to anybody on this globe. This charge of inferiority is an old dodge. It has been made available for oppression on many occasions. . . . For wherever men oppress their fellows, wherever they enslave them, they will endeavor to find the needed apology for such enslavement and oppression in the character of the people oppressed and enslaved. (Douglass 1865, p. 128)

One way that African Americans have combated the achievement gap ideology is by embracing education and intellectual development. Black culture highlights education as a means for social uplift. As a result, African Americans have struggled to obtain quality education from the early years of slavery to today. Theresa Perry (2003) argued that the Black community has developed a belief system and tradition of educational thought that act as a counter narrative to the achievement gap ideology. She describes this belief system as "freedom for literacy and literacy for freedom" (Perry 2003, p. 12). According to Perry, "you pursued learning because this is how you asserted yourself as a free person, how you claimed your humanity. You pursued learning so you could work for the racial uplift, for the liberation of your people. You pursued education so you could prepare yourself to lead your people" (Perry et al. 2003, p. 11).

As the achievement gap ideology developed and assumed celebrated myth status in the United States, African Americans grappled with the quest for racial uplift in a society that was bound to the idea of Black inferiority. The idealization of education was widely accepted. The key questions were how to obtain education and what kind of education Blacks should pursue to ensure benefits for the entire race. The debate on these topics is best summarized in the debate between those who supported liberal education for Blacks and those who argued for what would now be called vocational education.

Booker T. Washington believed that the way to produce the desired advancement of Black people was to support the interests of Whites. He argued that Blacks should be trained in practical skills and that they should use those skills to build economic strength. Washington believed that Whites would not oppose the success of Blacks if the success of Blacks was tied to their own economic success. The appropriate education for Blacks would be that of training to provide services that are useful and non-threatening to Whites. In Washington's words "The wisest among my race understand that the agitation of questions of social equality is the extremest folly, and that progress in the enjoyment of all the privileges that will come to us must be the result of severe and constant struggle rather that of artificial forcing" (Washington 1895, p. 184).

With time, Washington asserted, White people would come to accept the Black community's economic development. The next generation would benefit from the patience and efforts of the contemporary Blacks. Washington established the Tuskegee Institute, where he implemented his plan. Because Washington won the support of White leaders through his doctrine of conciliation, the Tuskegee Institute enjoyed abundant financial and political support.

Although Washington did not accept the doctrine that Blacks were inherently inferior, he seemed to embrace the ideas of social Darwinism. He believed that Blacks had to develop socially in order to be ready to take full advantage of civil rights. In his view, the Black race developed by living and working in close proximity to Whites. Blacks improved by emulating Whites.

> Put the black man where day by day he sees how the white man keeps his lawns, his windows; how he treats his wife and children and you will do more real helpful teaching than a whole library of lectures and sermons. . . . Practically all the real moral uplift the black people have got from whites—and this has been great indeed—has come from this observation of the white man's conduct. (Washington 1895, p. 197)

The belief that the growth and development of Blacks was dependent on the conciliation and emulation of Whites promoted the achievement gap ideology. This idea was embraced by many and continues to be evident in the discourse on the education of African Americans.

W. E. B. Du Bois, who would eventually teach at Washington's Tuskegee Institute, took a very different approach to education for the uplift of African Americans. Du Bois argued that Blacks should work for swift change. In Frederick Douglass's words, "power concedes nothing without a demand" (Hale 2001, p. 173). Du Bois rejected Washington's doctrine of conciliation saying instead, "We refuse to kiss the hands that smite us, but rather insist on striving by all civilized methods to keep wide educational opportunity, to keep the right to vote, to insist on equal civil rights and to gain every right and privilege open to a free American citizen" (Du Bois 1904, p. 331).

Du Bois was a staunch supporter of the liberal education of Blacks. He had attended Fisk University and valued the liberal education he had received. Du Bois believed that Black youth should be educated to assume leadership. He proposed that a "Talented Tenth" could be taught the skills to be social, political, and economic leaders. The talented tenth, once educated, could open opportunities for others. "If such opportunity were extended and broadened, a thousand times as many Negroes could join the ranks of the educated and able" (Du Bois 1945, p. 351).

Both Washington and Du Bois opposed segregation. However, they placed emphasis on different aspects of the problem. Washington argued that Blacks and Whites would benefit from integration because segregation was an unnatural social state that was detrimental to the survival of Southern society. He argued that segregation was unnecessary and it was a temptation to White men. His key argument for the purpose of Whites was that desegregation would not hurt White society but the continuation of legal segregation would stunt the development of Southern society (Washington 1895).

Du Bois took a different approach. He argued that integration was necessary for democracy, but he also recognized that being placed in schools with Whites would not solve all of the problems for Black children and the Black community. "To endure bad schools and wrong education because the schools are 'mixed' is a costly if not fatal mistake" (Du Bois 1935, p. 330). It was the responsibility of Black citizens to demand better and provide better for their children. However, the Black community also needed to begin to believe in its own worth and overcome the achievement gap ideology. In the absence of this change, integration would not benefit Black children.

"I have become curiously convinced," he wrote, "that until American Negroes believe in their own power and ability, they are going to be helpless before the white world, and the white world, realizing this inner paralysis and lack of self-confidence, is going to persist in its insane determination to rule the universe for its own selfish advantage" (Du Bois 1935, p. 333). In the meantime, Du Bois believed, the Black community should maintain a focus on ensuring that Black children received a quality liberal education in whatever school they attended.

Both Washington and Du Bois aided in the development of educational opportunities for African Americans. Their dialogue promoted support for Black colleges and universities, most of which offered some combination of vocational and liberal education. It was these institutions that produced teachers for Black schools. As a result, in some areas, teachers in Black schools possessed stronger credentials than their White counterparts (Siddle Walker 2001). African American teachers participated in their own professional organizations, pursued higher certifications, fought for longer school years, and discussed ways to promote desegregation.

While they accepted the idea that Blacks must grow socially, economically, and educationally to advance in American society, African American educators, like Du Bois, felt unsatisfied with the role education was expected to play in the lives of Black children.

> African American educators perceived that whites wanted blacks trained to read and write only at a level that they could fill the roles White employers needed for the menial positions they offered. . . . The philosophy of White communities about Blacks [was]: "We want Blacks to be mannerable, but not get to the point of being self-sufficient. (Siddle Walker 2001, p. 761)

The ideas of both Booker T. Washington and W. E. B. Du Bois demonstrate the pragmatism that is prevalent in African American beliefs about education. Although they approached the education of Blacks in different ways, Du Bois and Washington both advocated the swift and direct training of African Americans. They did not spend time quibbling over the different pedagogical theories of their time. Their ideas demonstrated a focus on the efficient and effectual training and education of Blacks for social uplift as opposed to individual fulfillment.

Chapter 2

Traditional and Emerging Research on the Achievement Gap

Research studies demonstrate that an outcome gap exists between African Americans and Whites. Standardized IQ tests show an average of a 15-point gap between the scores of Whites and those of Blacks. Analyses of the National Education Longitudinal Study (NELS) have shown that a gap exists in the graduation rates, income levels, college entrance rates, college completion rates, and employment rates of Whites and Blacks (Burnham, 1985; Herrnstein and Murray, 1994; Pino and Smith, 2004; Singham, 2003). Results of the National Assessment of Educational Progress (NAEP) demonstrate that African American children are on average four years behind their White peers by the end of high school (Foster 2005). The outcome gap begins in kindergarten and grows throughout the years of schooling.

Research on the achievement gap has yielded an abundance of descriptive statistics to show that Whites outperform Blacks on all standardized tests of ability and achievement. These statistics are used to predict and justify the continued underachievement of African American children. They support the achievement gap ideology with scientific data just was done in the past. In this chapter, I will provide an overview of the progression of research on the achievement gap. This is not designed to provide a comprehensive or exhaustive review of literature on the test score gap.

Traditional explanations of and responses to the outcome gap fall into two categories. The first category is one that I will call the "conservative" traditional view. I use the term "conservative" to identify this view with those who promote the ideals of individualism, personal responsibility (pulling oneself up by one's own bootstraps), capitalism, the Puritan work ethic, meritocracy, and limited government interference in private affairs. The conservative traditional view of the outcome gap is rather simplistic in nature. Simply put, this view is that African Americans do not achieve because they do not have the intellectual ability, collective will, or moral proclivity to do what it takes to succeed. They, essentially, are the cause of their own problems.

I will call the second category the "liberal" traditional view. The term "liberal" connotes the ideals of cooperation, social responsibility, socialism, fundamental rights, and government involvement for the "common good." The traditional liberal view of the achievement gap is far more complex though equally grounded in the achievement gap ideology. To state this view plainly, African Americans do not achieve because they cannot do any better, but it's not their fault. Outside forces (social, economic, or cultural) cause them to fail. Both of these views have existed throughout the existence of the achievement gap ideology. At different periods either the conservative or the liberal view has been more prominent.

Traditional research on the outcome gap stemmed from the nation's need to address what was known as the "Negro problem." Some of the first true research studies aimed at determining the educational needs of Black children were conducted to support or refute segregation. Previously, research focused on whether Black children could benefit from education as opposed to how students should be educated. In numerous cases aimed at overturning legal segregation, Thurgood Marshall and the NAACP legal team used research studies to demonstrate that Black children were harmed by segregated schooling (Marshall, 1954).

In the *Brown v. Board of Education* case, Marshall presented research that had been conducted using Black and White dolls. Young Black children were asked which doll they would prefer. Invariably, the children preferred to play with the White doll. The researchers concluded that the segregated conditions in which the students lived caused poor self-esteem among the Black children.

Although the *Brown v. Board* decision did not rest exclusively on the research that was presented, the arguments made by the plaintiffs and the final decision had a significant impact on the future of research on African American education. The Supreme Court decided that separate schools were "inherently unequal" because segregated schools did not allow Black children to develop the social networks and connections necessary for future success. Segregation, according to the court, also disadvantaged Black children by communicating that they were inferior to White children. Once again, the idea was posited that Black children would benefit from being in the presence of and learning from Whites. Although, in many ways, the *Brown v. Board* decision furthered the cause of racial equality, the desegregation of schools also set the stage for the growth of the outcome gap and the breathed new life into the achievement gap ideology.

During the period of segregation, lower outcomes for Blacks in segregated schools were assumed. It was well known that schools for Blacks were under-funded (Siddle Walker, 2001). Black children were often forced to walk long distances past nearby White schools to attend school in substandard buildings with old books and no supplies. Given these conditions, Black underachievement was expected by White leaders. Siddle Walker (2001) argues that Black teachers and principals in many areas were more highly educated than their White counterparts. Despite the lack of resources, the students received a high quality of education from teachers who cared for the children, were part of their community, communicated freely with their families, and understood the needs of African American children.

When Black children began to be integrated into White schools, the achievement gap ideology became even more important and the outcome gap became evident. Although some assumed that Black children would improve their performance if they were educated alongside White children, Black children remained less successful than their White counterparts. Black children were taken out of their own schools to enter White schools that were not designed to meet their needs. The well-qualified African American teachers were not given positions in the integrated schools. Their knowledge and commitment were lost from the public school system (Siddle Walker, 2001). African American children were now taught by teachers who were more or less hostile to Blacks, were outsiders to their community, and only understood Black children as a contrast to White children.

By the mid 1960s, researchers were spending a significant about of time researching the underachievement of Blacks in schools. The Coleman Report (1966), a study commissioned by the Civil Rights Act of 1964 to determine the cause of the educational disparities between Blacks and Whites, concluded that schools had little influence over the educational outcomes of children. Instead, the educational success of children was predicted by family background. Daniel Patrick Moynihan, in a 1965 report, also found family background to be the main factor in the underachievement of Blacks. He identified what he called a crisis in the Black family that was causing poverty, destructive behavior, and low educational achievement (Hallinan, 2001). These studies represented the beginning of the liberal traditional research on Black education.

In 1970, the conservative traditional approach to researching the outcome gap was strengthened by the reemergence of biological determinism, the idea that the underachievement of Blacks was due to an inherent lack of intelligence. Arthur M. Jensen (1973) researched the IQ and achievement scores of Blacks and Whites. He concluded that the lack of educational achievement among Blacks was due to "their limited mental abilities and their likely low-level future occupations" (Hallinan, 2001, p. 3). Jensen argued that there was little educators could due to change the intellectual abilities of Black students. It would be better for schools to offer different types of learning to Blacks to prepare them for their likely station in life.

Liberal traditionalists countered this argument by asserting that the standardized tests were culturally biased. Cultural deprivation theory and cultural difference theory were advanced to explain that Black children could not achieve in school because their culture did not match the culture of White society or the public school classroom. The specific types of abilities that were measured by intelligence tests were determined by culture. Blacks did not have access to the same cultural background that was a prerequisite for success on the tests (Hallinan, 2001).

If Black student achievement was low due to the fact that their culture was different, one might induce that the way to improve it would be to change the culture of Blacks so that it closely resembled that of Whites. Traditional liberal educators have taken that approach. By implementing programs such as Head Start and Title I, traditional liberal educators have attempted to compensate for the cultural deprivation of Black children by providing additional time and resources to socialize and remediate Black children. It appears that this approach was at least partly successful as the outcome gap was diminished between 1970 and 1980.

During this period, traditional liberal researchers studied in great depths the difference between Blacks and Whites in order to explain the lack of Black student achievement. Researchers determined that the breakdown of the Black family, the prevalence of female-headed households, the incidence of poverty, and the size of Black families were catalysts in the outcome gap (Hallinan, 2001; Jencks, 1972; Moynihan, 1995; Sewell and Hauser 1975). Liberal researchers during this time also determined that elements of Black culture explained the outcome gap. John Ogbu (1978) identified what he termed as "oppositional culture." In his view, African American children were trained to act in opposition to White culture. This was their way of coping with their oppression.

Later, Ogbu along with Signithia Fordham (1986) expounded on this idea by arguing that African American young people consider doing well in school to be "acting White." African American children would reject school success as their response to oppression. Ogbu (1978) believed that African Americans were different in this respect from other minorities in that they were involuntary minorities. As such, he argued, African Americans found little connection between their efforts to receive a quality education and the economic and social rewards of education. Unfortunately, Ogbu's research contributed to the achievement gap ideology by connecting the outcome gap to the cultural characteristics of the Black race.

By the 1980s, under the leadership of President Ronald Reagan, the conservative traditional view made great strides. The 1983 *A Nation at Risk* report played a major role in shifting the focus of educators from achieving educational equality to focusing on educational excellence. This shift in focus ended the progress being made in closing the gap. Politicians and educators began to once again focus on identifying students who possessed desirable characteristics and focusing resources on those students. Middle- and upper-class Whites promoted the development of programs for students labeled as gifted and talented (Wells & Crain, 1997). Students received this prestigious label based on their scores on standardized IQ and achievement tests and teacher recommendation. In accordance with the achievement gap ideology, Black students seldom if ever participated in these programs.

With the question of segregation and overt racism considered settled by the mid 1980s, conservative traditional researchers and theorists found it particularly easy to once again advance the idea that school achievement or the lack thereof was due to innate intelligence. Placement in the gifted track was based on intelligence scores. If Black children were not able to produce high intelligence and achievement scores, they were not entitled to participate in these programs. It was simply a matter of fact that students with less intelligence would not perform as well in school. Based on the outcomes of standardized tests since desegregation, conservative theorists postulated, Black students were simply less intelligent than White students (Burnham, 1985). Numerous studies were conducted to describe what was termed the "Black-White score gap" (Hallinan, 2001).

In 1994, Richard Herrnstein and Charles Murray gave full voice to the conservative traditional view of the nature and origin of the outcome gap (Herrnstein and Murray, 1994). In so doing, they advanced the most complete and accepted arguments for the achievement gap ideology. They also made the idea of the normal curve part of the popular consciousness. Their book, *The Bell Curve* (1994), spent 15 weeks on the *New York Times* Best Seller List.

Herrnstein and Murray (1994) argued that the differences in the educational, social, and economic outcomes of Whites and Blacks are due to authentic differences in the intellectual abilities of the racial groups. They showed what they believed to be correlations between ability test scores and outcomes such as educational attainment, income, welfare dependency, crime, and parenting behaviors. According to the study, people with lower IQ scores have lower educational attainment, lower income, higher rates of welfare dependency, higher incidents of crime, and poorer parenting behaviors. This is true for all people according to the study. Almost all of the differences displayed by racial and ethnic groups could be accounted for by differences in IQ.

In addition, Herrstein and Murray argued that IQ scores are determined largely by heredity. Unfortunately for African Americans, their study postulates that Blacks are on average less intelligent than Whites. "Translated into centiles, this means that the average white person tests higher than about 84 percent of the population of blacks and that the average black person tests higher than about 16 percent of whites" (Herrnstein and Murray, 1994, p. 269). Based on this, the researchers argued that the outcome gap is due to the inherent intellectual inferiority of Blacks. They went on to argue that social policies such as affirmative action and compensatory education would not alleviate the problems of the outcome gap. Instead, resources should be focused on developing the abilities of the most able and finding appropriate jobs and roles for people who were less able.

Liberal traditional researchers and African American leaders fired back against Herrnstein and Murray's findings, but they were unable to eliminate the influence of the study. At best, the great outcry against *The Bell Curve* served to confine those who agreed with the achievement gap ideology to discussing it among themselves to avoid being called racist. Unfortunately, the achievement gap ideology continued to be as strong as ever.

The 1990s brought about a shift from the focus on the achievement gap based on race to the idea of the achievement gap as an issue of poverty. For this reason, researchers began to use terms such as "at-risk," "urban," "inner-city," "underclass," "disadvantaged," and "diverse" instead of racial terms. Numerous studies have demonstrated that race is correlated to income and that both race and socioeconomic status are correlated to achievement. As a result, some researchers argue that the cause of underachievement is poverty instead of race. This argument is pleasing to both conservative and liberal traditionalists.

A focus on poverty as the cause of the gap releases both conservatives and liberals from responsibility for confronting the issue of race. This frees traditional liberals to focus efforts to close the achievement gap on eliminating poverty or ameliorating its effects. On the other hand, the focus on poverty allows traditional conservatives to consider the achievement gap to be a mere side effect of capitalism. Conservatives argue that the outcome gap is tangible proof that American society is a meritocracy. If people do not want to be poor, they must work hard and get a good education. Children are poor because their parents have not done this. This is unavoidable, conservatives would argue, in a meritocratic society.

The attempt to steer attention away from race has contributed to the rise of the ideal of "color-blindness." Color-blindness is based on the idea that the way to eliminate the problems related to the concept of race is to eliminate all attention to race in society and to act as though race has no effect on outcomes. This leads to arguments against measures aimed at addressing the issues of racism and discrimination.

Affirmative action programs, "race-based" scholarships and college admission policies, African American political organizations, and public school desegregation plans have all come under fire based on the idea that race should never be a consideration in a color-blind society. The rhetoric of color-blindness includes statements denying personal racism such as "I don't see color" and "I don't even notice that you're Black." It also includes denials of the existence and effects of racism and discrimination such as "They are just playing the race card," "It happened 200 years ago, get over it" and "Race doesn't matter anymore."

One might argue that color-blindness should be the goal of a free society because it is the only way to eliminate the specter of race from our society. However, color-blindness does not negate racism. Consider the following story:

During the war, the armies laid land mines in a field that separated the two enemy camps. The mines were spaced systematically and at varying distances so that no one could successfully tread through the field without a detailed map showing the layout of the mines. Neither army possessed a complete map. Each could only avoid the mines they had set. When the war ended, both the victors and the conquered ignored the field, too engrossed in rebuilding their own lands and reclaiming their economies to devote time to removing the mines. A generation of people lived separated by and in fear of the mines.

As the years passed, the land mines became overgrown and the signs that warned people that they were entering a danger zone faded. To successive generations, tales of the mines became less and less significant—simply reminders of a time that everyone should just "get over" or forget. Over time, it became easy to believe that the land mines were simply features of the landscape. A few people were even able to successfully cross the field. Those few were lauded as examples to the others.

Those who stubbornly pointed out that there were landmines in the field were faulted for living in the past, looking for danger where none existed, and using the past as an excuse for their own laziness or hatred. They were told that they could leave the past behind anytime they wanted by just crossing the field. Then, one day, the government and its representatives from both of the previously warring parties made a proclamation that land mines were a thing of the past and separation was no longer desirable. With great fanfare, they declared that the field was now a park. It was time to send the children out to play!

Eliminating all reference to race and advocating color-blindness in a society that was founded and built on race and the achievement gap ideology is like carefully laying out landmines in a field, then burying them under a layer of dirt and sod and sending the children out to play. American society has taken centuries to construct race in such a way that racism is evident throughout American institutions. The structures of institutional racism, including the achievement gap ideology, have been grounded in the day to day life of our society. They cannot be removed simply by proclamation.

With the passage of the No Child Left Behind Act of 2001, new emphasis was focused on the outcome gap and the achievement gap ideology. The No Child Left Behind Act (NCLB) required that states test all students in grades 3 through 8 in reading and mathematics and that the results of the tests be disaggregated by race and income as well as other factors. The law raised the stakes for local school districts to ensure strong educational outcomes for African American students by requiring that schools and school districts be judged based on the academic performance of students overall as well as the academic performance of each definable "subgroup" including African American students, Hispanic students, and low-income students along with others. As a result, many schools that previously had a reputation of being "good" schools were labeled as failing because of the low test scores of their African American, low-income, and limited English-proficient students.

In addition, schools began to focus more attention, curriculum initiatives, classroom instruction, special programs, and funding on the needs of students who were struggling in reading and math. By the time of reauthorization, states and local school districts were lobbying for the law to be changed or eliminated. Under pressure from lobbyists, teachers' unions, state education officials, and parents, both the Republicans and Democrats who originally supported the law began to call for changes.

By 2007, the doctrine of color-blindness had become widely promoted. On June 28, 2007, the U.S. Supreme Court struck down the desegregation plans of school districts in Seattle, Washington, and Louisville, Kentucky, ruling that the Constitution is "color-blind" and disallows any use of race by the government unless the government can demonstrate a "compelling interest" in using race. In the 5–4 decision, the majority argued that there was no proven educational benefit inherent in diversity, that integration is not proven to improve the academic achievement of Black children, and that the school districts have "no compelling interest" in ensuring diversity in public schools.

The crux of the argument was that government does not have a compelling interest in remedying de facto segregation (Roberts, 2007). Therefore, the government may not use racial categories in making decisions even if it is for the purpose of promoting diversity or eliminating segregation or discrimination. This opinion has made color-blindness the rule of law and set the stage for challenges of all government programs aimed at promoting diversity and integration.

The end of the 20th century and the dawn of a new millennium spawned a new generation of research on the education of African Americans. This research, still grounded in the achievement gap ideology, seeks to determine how African Americans are different from White students and how these differences cause Black underachievement. Studies have been conducted to investigate the motivational patterns, peer relationships, family dynamics, beliefs about education, and academic decisions of African American youth. All of these studies compared African American youth to Whites.

More recent studies have taken on the task of investigating instances of the outcome gap and community reactions to the gap. John Ogbu (2003) conducted research in an affluent suburban community in Ohio. The researcher participated in school community-based initiatives to investigate the presence of an outcome gap in the community. Ogbu conducted interviews with students, teachers, parents, administrators, and community members. He found that people were generally frustrated and felt as though they were doing everything right. Many of the African American community members felt as though the attention being focused on the outcome gap was designed to embarrass the Black community. John Ogbu (2003) concluded that the outcome gap stemmed from many factors, but he identified the factor that he termed "academic disengagement" as the most important factor.

Amy Stuart Wells and Robert Crain (1997) studied students in an urban area in the Midwest. The school district had been ordered to create a desegregation plan. Wells and Crain conducted interviews with students, parents, and school personnel to gather information about the color line as it existed in the district. They found specific differences between the Black students who transferred schools to attend more affluent schools and students who refused to leave the poorly funded local schools. They found that the students who transferred schools and were subsequently more successful had parents who were intimately involved in making strategic decisions about their children's education. In this way, they were similar to the middle-class Whites in the study.

Traditional research on the outcome gap and the education of African Americans has served to strengthen the achievement gap ideology. Most studies have focused on using quantitative data to describe the outcome gap and devising theories to explain and/or justify its existence. Qualitative studies have often revolved around comparing the responses of African Americans to those of Whites. The differences in the responses have been used to explain Black underachievement. There is no doubt that traditional research has provided an abundance of information about the ways in which African Americans differ from Whites. Unfortunately, this research has contributed little to the elimination of the outcome gap, and it has only strengthened the achievement gap ideology in American society.

EMERGING RESEARCH ALTERNATIVES

Supporters of quality education for African Americans have begun to take alternative approaches to researching the outcome gap and its origins. One important trend has been the increase in the number of African American researchers taking on the task of investigating quality education for African American children. Another important trend has been that of thinking critically about the role of race in American society and public education. Finally, there has been an emerging trend of devoting resources to studying success instead of failure.

African American researchers have advanced research that gathers information about the African American community from the African American community. As opposed to comparing African Americans to Whites, these researchers investigate and illuminate African American culture, views, and needs in their own right. Theresa Perry researched African American attitudes about education and noted the ways in which recurring themes of Black culture support the education of African American children (Perry, Steele, and Hilliard, 2003). She explained that the struggle for education is an important theme. "This explicit, and continually articulated belief system functions as a counternarrative, one that stands in opposition to the dominant society's notions about the intellectual capacity of African Americans, the role of learning in their lives, the meaning and purpose of school, and the power of their intellect" (Perry et al. 2003, p. 49).

She focuses on the ways in which schools can meet the needs of Black children. Perry argues that African American student achievement is far more complicated in the post-Civil Rights era. She suggests that schools could be made into "figured universes" in which African American students were engaged in a culture of achievement (Perry et al. 2003).

Other African American researchers such as Vanessa Siddle-Walker, Theresa Perry, Lisa Delpit, and Gloria Ladson-Billings have contributed a growing knowledge base on quality education for African American children. The contributions of these researchers are unique because the researchers do not see African American culture as disadvantaged or pathological in any way. They have the opportunity to gain access to the African American community in ways in which White researchers often cannot. In addition, these African American educators share the sense of pragmatism that is a hallmark of African American culture.

The focus of their research is less on creating a theory about the origin of the problem and more on finding practical and meaningful solutions to the problem. This does not mean that White researchers cannot successfully conduct research on the education of African American children. It simply means that African American researchers provide an important and necessary perspective.

Thinking critically about the role of race in society and schools is another trend in emerging research about the education of African Americans. Critical race theory developed out of the legal profession. Critical race theorists advocate racial realism, the idea that racism is more than a state of mind. It is the way in which society doles out power and privilege. Critical race theory can be described as pessimistic when it comes to the elimination of racism. It posits that empathy and generosity do not truly exist in politics. Advancements in equal treatment for people of color and other oppressed populations are based on people in power making decisions to protect or promote their own interests (Bell, 1992). This premise of interest convergence is a hallmark of critical race theory.

Derrick Bell (2004) explains the two rules of interest convergence:

Rule 1. The interest of blacks in achieving racial equality will be accommodated only when that interest converges with the interests of whites in policy-making positions. This convergence is far more important for gaining relief than the degree of harm suffered by blacks or the character of proof offered to prove that harm.

Rule 2. Even when interest-convergence results in an effective racial remedy, that remedy will be abrogated at the point that policymakers fear the remedial policy is threatening the superior societal status of whites, particularly those in the middle and upper classes. (p. 69)

Critical race theory provides researchers with a different lens through which to view the history of African American education.

When one considers the history of African American education through the lens of critical race theory, it is easy to see that the limited advances in the provision of education to African Americans have been due in large part to arguments being made for the connection of the fortunes of African Americans with those of Whites. Indeed, Booker T. Washington's beliefs in conciliation were based on the same idea. By promoting the ways in which helping Blacks could benefit Whites, Washington essentially used the idea of interest convergence to gain support for his efforts. Similarly, Derrick Bell (2004) theorizes that the *Brown v. Board* decision was based on interest convergence. Improving relationships with Blacks became important for policymakers due to their need to improve America's image in the world.

The *Brown v. Board* case provided policymakers with the opportunity to meet this need. Later, when the interests of Whites and Blacks were no longer so clearly and closely connected, the court began to scale back the influence of its ruling. Bell's views are again supported by the court's decision regarding desegregation and integration plans in public elementary schools. Critical race theory is an important concept because it focuses on understanding the social/political construct of race and the ways in which it influences policy, espoused values, law and the actions of individuals and groups.

PEDAGOGICAL APPROACHES FOR EXCELLENCE IN EDUCATION

The Negro needs neither segregated schools nor mixed schools. What he needs is Education. (Du Bois, 1938, p. 335)

The premise upon which public education for African Americans was conceived is faulty. Our educational system continues to operate under the assumptions of Black inferiority. Most of the pedagogical approaches advocated for Blacks involve increased remediation. The attempt is to make up for the perceived academic and intellectual deficits of African Americans. Black students are treated as though they have low-average intelligence. They are placed in special education and intervention programs where they receive direct instruction on a range of low-level skills that are often unrelated to the skills, attitudes, and behaviors that are necessary in school and life. Children in these programs may eventually gain the rudimentary skills necessary to complete the remedial programs, but during their time in the programs they lose access to the grade-level skills necessary for the successful completion of school.

The learning style that is preferred by many African Americans is associated in public schools with low intelligence. African Americans tend to be field-dependent learners. They tend to have a more kinesthetic learning style (Hale, 2001). Blacks are more likely, according to research, to have an external locus of control and to prefer direct instruction. This may be because of the Black community's sense of pragmatism about education. In general, African Americans want to be taught by someone.

African Americans place great value on roles of authority and feel that authority is important in the teacher-student relationship. The more the liberal educators advocate moving toward discovery and inquiry learning with teachers assuming the role of facilitator instead of authority figure, the more alienated and lost Black students feel in schools (Delpit, 1993). Educators must stop assuming that what is theoretically pleasing for educating White middle-class students will get the same reaction and results from students with a different way of life.

Lisa Delpit, in her work entitled *Other People's Children: Cultural Conflict in the Classroom* (1993), explains this in more detail. She argues that liberal educators promote practices that may not necessarily support the success of Black students. According to Delpit, Black children need to learn to operate in a culture of power. To deny children this knowledge is to handicap them in relating in mainstream society. "To provide schooling for everyone's children that reflects liberal, middle-class values and aspirations is to ensure the maintenance of the status quo, to ensure that power, the culture of power, remains in the hands of those who already have it" (Delpit, 1993, p 28).

Power relationships are acted out in public schools (Delpit, 1993). Those children who come to school with an understanding of the dominant culture have a distinct advantage. Not only do they know how to interact appropriately in the school environment, but they are also accepted by teachers and others in authority. African American children who have not been explicitly taught specific elements of the dominant culture are often confused by what they perceive as mixed messages. This is particularly the case when it comes to teaching style and matters of discipline.

Teachers who exercise power passively often find that African American children do not respond to their requests (Delpit, 1993). African American students frequently report that teachers who choose to facilitate instead of direct do not care about students and are unable to control the classroom. They possess much greater respect for teachers they label as strict, caring, and in charge.

Colleges of education, administrators, and practicing teachers support the maintenance of the status quo by equating students' ethnic, racial, and socioeconomic status with failure and underachievement. For educators, Black students are at-risk. This assumption makes it acceptable for African American children to underachieve without teachers and schools being to blame.

We expose student teachers to an education that relies upon name-calling and labeling ("disadvantaged," "at-risk," "learning disabled," "the underclass") to explain its failures, and calls upon research study after research study to inform teachers that school achievement is intimately and inevitably linked with socioeconomic status. . . . In other words, we teach teachers rationales for failure, not visions of success. (Delpit, 1993, p. 178)

The response to these different needs and pragmatic view of educations is culturally relevant teaching. Advocated by Gloria Ladson-Billings (1994), culturally relevant pedagogy has some important hallmarks. Her vision of the culturally relevant school includes providing "educational self-determination," "honor and respect [for the] students' home culture," and helping "African American students understand the world as it is and equip[ping] them to change it for the better" (Ladson-Billings, 1994, p. 137, 138, 139). In order to help students succeed, teachers must support African American students in ways that are relevant to their way of life. For Ladson-Billings, the specific teaching techniques are less important than the beliefs of teachers and the extent to which they create a connection with African American students.

Janice Hale (2001) asserts that teachers must be made aware of specific characteristics of African American learners. They should be taught to recognize the characteristics of African American learners, particularly boys, as normal. In addition, they should be taught about the strengths of African American children including oral communication, kinesthetic activity, and affective orientation (Hale, 2001).

The voices of African American educators, researchers, parents, and community members are critically important in the quest to improve the quality of education for African American youth. These voices can create a new conversation about meeting student and community needs. The next chapter will explore research methods that can be used to engage in the dialogue with African Americans community members about educating African American youth.

Chapter 3

Engaging in the Dialogue

"Orature represents the total body of oral discourses, styles and traditions of a people. Attempts to understand African American orature have failed because they misconstrue the nature and character of African American discourse, written or spoken. Often ignorant of African philosophy and culture, commentators have imposed Western constructs and values on material that grows out of coherent, albeit different, traditions. The result has been a failure to understand or value that material as well as an inability to recognize or correct that failure."

—Asante, 1998, p. 25

Research on African American education and eliminating the outcome gap should focus on the following:

• Opening a discourse that is not based in and predicated upon Whiteness
• Engaging in a dialogue with the former object of the discussion (shifting from viewing Black children as objects to understanding them as subjects and bringing the Black community into the dialogue as stakeholders, leaders, and experts)
• Investigating the problem with the purpose of solving it in a practical sense instead of justifying its existence.

In this chapter, I discuss the methods I have used to engage in a dialogue with African American community members. First, I discuss issues that hinder valid research with African American community members. Then, I provide examples of quality research studies that provide meaningful information about African American education. I go on to explain the reasoning for my approach to this study and the principles used in my research design.

I include a list of the research participants and a description of the analysis process.

In order to design schools for the success of African American children, educational leaders must step outside of a mentality of Whiteness. As opposed to considering the characteristics of African American learners with the expectation that they mirror those of Whites and mainstream society, educational leaders and researchers must consider African American students in their own right. Researchers must recognize that African American children are members of a community with its own history and its own set of beliefs, values, and traditions. Researchers must also recognize that, as a rule, African Americans place little trust in research. This is particularly the case for quantitative research.

As a general rule, African American culture places far more emphasis on narrative and personal experience. Although this may hinder attempts to engage a large sample of African Americans in a correlational or experimental study, it may actually aid in engaging African Americans in the kinds of research that validates their thoughts, ideas, and experiences. Researchers may also find that quantitative research provides them with little useful information that educational practitioners can use. This is because quantitative research is almost exclusively based on a comparison to a control group, in most cases either Whites or those minorities that are considered to be most mainstream or reflective of White middle-class culture. This kind of research places African Americans at the disadvantage of being thought of as the object being acted upon. This kind of research may be useful to substantiate or challenge a theory or hypothesis. However, because we have so little useful information about meeting the educational needs of African Americans, it is highly unlikely that hypotheses framed in Whiteness would be helpful in learning about these needs.

Given the lack of understanding provided by traditional research on the cultural characteristics of African Americans, research should be conducted in ways that better coincide with the beliefs and cultural characteristics of the participants. Open-ended research techniques have the potential to shed some light on the needs of African Americans in education. These techniques can provide researchers who are outside of the African American culture with some basic knowledge about the culture, beliefs, and traditions inherent in African American culture. This is essential because the greatest barrier to quality education for African Americans is the inability or unwillingness to "see" African Americans as something other than disadvantaged, pathological versions of the White middle class. As a result, traditionally, African Americans are seen as either lazy people who do not take advantage of the opportunities placed before them or as helpless victims of a society they are ill-equipped to handle. Neither of these ways of thinking allows a clear picture of African American students.

EXAMPLES OF QUALITY RESEARCH ON AFRICAN AMERICAN EDUCATION

Recently, researchers have begun to gather information through in depth interviews with African Americans. Schwitzer et al. (1999) interviewed successful African American college students to learn about their adjustment to college. This research yielded a model describing the factors affecting college adjustment including feelings of isolation, incidences of racism, and difficulty in approaching faculty. Diamond and Gomez's (2004) interview of middle-class and working-class African American parents about their perceptions of schools yielded a comparison of the ways in which middle-class and working-class parents approach involvement in schools.

One particularly rich area of inquiry is the perceptions of African American students. Honora (2003), Howard (2002), and Wasonga and Christman (2003) each conducted qualitative research to determine African American students' perceptions of schools and teachers. Honora's (2003) research was based on prior research results indicating that students' lack of identification with school is "one of the many explanations for discrepancies in school achievement" (p. 58). Honora found that low-achieving and high-achieving African American students were likely to identify with school socially rather than academically. However, high-achieving African American females were most likely to identify school as a place to gain knowledge. The students' perceptions were strongly related to the feedback they received from teachers.

Howard (2002) investigated elementary and secondary school students' descriptions of effective and ineffective teachers. Howard identified three characteristics of teachers perceived to be effective by African American students. These included establishing family and community environments, caring, and providing verbal affirmation (Howard, 2002).

Numerous studies have focused on African American adolescents' and young adults' beliefs about school and educational achievement and have yielded findings regarding African American student motivation, relationships with teachers and peers, and future aspirations (Hebert 1998, Howard 2003, Hwang, Echols & Vrongistinos 2002, Sanders 1997). In addition, an increasing outcome gap between African American males and other groups has led to a variety of studies about improving the performance of African American males in the school system (Noguera 2003, Benson 2000, Jordan &

Cooper 2003). These studies investigate reasons for the underachievement of African American males in relation to other groups.

Conchas (2006) investigated the concept of race among "high-achieving urban youth" through a case study of a high school. He combined interviews, focus groups, observation, and quantitative analysis of survey data. This new wave of qualitative research studies has begun to provide information about African Americans from African Americans. They have investigated issues related to both African American student failure and success and they have offered ideas for policymakers and educators. However, to date, an extensive search has not yielded qualitative studies aimed at accessing the current African American discourse on education in light of the achievement gap.

RESEARCH DESIGN AND METHODOLOGY

The only viable way to determine how to meet the needs of African American children is to go to the source. "If we want to know how people felt, what they experienced, what they remembered, what their emotions and motives were like and the reasons for acting as they did—why not just ask them?" (Wilcox quoted in Vaughn, Schumm, and Sinagub, 1996, p. 18). To gain knowledge that is useful in combating the outcome gap and the achievement gap ideology, culturally sensitive ethnographic research is key. Specifically, a researcher should use a research design that utilizes prolonged dialogue. This will allow participants to explore their thoughts on education and the outcome gap. Practitioners and researchers can greatly benefit from accessing the African American community's practical and values-based discourse about education through culturally sensitive research.

Molefi Asante (1998) argued that Eurocentric research methods, defined as methods grounded in European or White beliefs, values, and ways of knowing, are invalid methods for conducting research on African Americans. Indeed, in his view, the only way to extract oneself from the Eurocentric ideas is to locate oneself firmly in the Afrocentric viewpoint. Asante makes bold statements about the use of research in oppression by discussing Eurocentric research as "hierarchical discourse." Hierarchical discourse, according to Asante (1998), seeks to control the societal discourse by "defining not only the terms of discussion but also the grounds upon which the discussion will be waged" (p. 34). Hierarchical discourse is also used to control who engages in the discourse by forcing all would-be participants to undergo "initiation." Only those who accept the structural patterns, values, and beliefs receive initiation by the established order. Those who are not initiated or who oppose the dominant discourse are stifled.

Most research is located firmly within the realm of hierarchical Eurocentric discourse. Asante argues that people of African descent must assert their own freedom by conducting their own research. To do this, the researchers must reject Eurocentric values and beliefs.

Afrocentric research ideals are built on foundational beliefs and values of the African American culture. One hallmark of these ideals is the rejection of objectivity as an ideal. Afrocentric research embraces the idea that "all analysis is culturally centered and flows from ideological assumptions" (Asante, 1987, p. 159).

Afrocentric research also embraces a unique view of the role of the researchers. In Afrocentric research paradigm, the researcher is actually a researcher/activist whose responsibility is both to understand and to empower. The Afrocentric researcher must answer to the community as well as to other researchers (Milam, 1992).

Asante and other researchers have rejected research methodologies such as quantitative analysis as Eurocentric because of the separation they place between the researcher and participant and the reliance on objectivity. Afrocentrists promote more open-ended strategies such as in-depth interviews and case studies. Unfortunately, Asante provides no specific guidance on designing Afrocentric research studies or analyzing data.

Linda Tillman (2002) advocates what she has termed "culturally sensitive research approaches" as valid and meaningful ways to engage in research with African Americans. Building on the principles of Afrocentrism espoused by Asante and others, Tillman advocates a research paradigm that embraces the historical practice of African American scholars. "Today, the concerns of Du Bois, Cooper, and Woodson are still relevant when considering the consequences of the privileging of voice and unequal power relations in educational research. In the absence of culturally sensitive research approaches, there will continue to be a void in what the larger research community knows and understands about the education of African Americans" (Tillman, 2002, p. 4).

Research with African Americans must address the role that culture plays in the research and analysis process. Culturally sensitive research practices have four basic hallmarks. As described by Tillman, culturally sensitive research practices include "culturally congruent research methods," which primarily consist of open ended interview, and observational techniques and the use of culturally specific knowledge as parts of the research process.

Tillman describes what she calls "cultural resistance to theoretical dominance" as another key component of culturally sensitive research practices. This idea incorporates the practice of questioning and confronting power relationships in research theory and practice and making African American culture central to the research. Culturally sensitive research practices provide more guidance on data analysis by highlighting culturally sensitive data interpretations and culturally informed theory and practice. Tillman (2002) notes that the interpretation of data should be a joint process between the researcher and participant that recognizes "experiential knowledge as legitimate, appropriate, and necessary for analyzing, understanding, and reporting data" (p. 6).

The Council on Research in Black Education (CORIBE), a division of the American Educational Research Association (of which Linda Tillman is a member), established principles for research on Black education in their "Transformative Research and Action Agenda for the New Century." The principles advanced by CORIBE include centering research perspectives on the African "ethnic family," prioritizing the ethnic family over the individual, "differential use of three modes of response to domination and hegemony: (a) Adaptation—adopting what is deemed useful; (b) Improvisation—substituting or improvising alternatives that are more sensitive to our culture; and (c) Resistance—resisting that which is destructive and not in the best interests of our people" (King 2005, 20). In addition, the CORIBE principles focus on developing understanding instead of seeking facts and "truth," ensuring research validity, using research to inform practice, and vice versa and wielding influence over the destiny of the ethnic family.

Finally, the CORIBE principles advance two essential beliefs. First, education is a human right and, second, in the words of Joyce King (2005), "African people are not empty vessels. We are not new to the study of and practice of education and socialization that is rooted in deep thought. We will not accept a dependent status in the approach and solution to our problems" (p. 21). These principles, along with those of Afrocentric research and the culturally sensitive research framework, provide the framework for this research.

The following questions serve as the focus of this study:

- How do African American community members describe education that meets the needs of African American students?
- How do African American community members conceive of parent, educator, and community roles in the education of Black children?
- How do African American community members analyze the achievement gap?

As I began to consider ways to gather information about African American community member's views, my goal was to gather and represent the information in a way that respects and represents my culture and that of the participants. The Culturally Sensitive Research Framework best reflects and honors African American intellectual tradition.

I conducted a series of ethnographic interviews with 15 African American adults. The participants were drawn from a network of African Americans from ethnically and socioeconomically diverse communities within the state of Illinois. I first attempted to identify participants for the study through a local community college because of the wide range of community members served in this setting. However, this attempt yielded only one individual who was willing to participate solely based on announcements in the school newsletter and posters and flyers. The community college was not willing to provide lists of African American students or to target African American students for a direct e-mail campaign. Faced with this difficulty, I altered my recruitment strategy to better reflect African American culture and my personal interactions with other African Americans.

Instead of trying to identify participants as an unknown researcher, I used my personal networks to make connections with a larger number of potential participants. I contacted three African American women in my social network explaining my research and asking them to refer people who might be willing to participate. I stipulated that I needed to interview men and women between the ages of 20 and 40. The three women went immediately into action calling and e-mailing friends, family members, sorority sisters, coworkers, and others. Within two days, I had 30 individuals volunteering to meet with me.

With this pool of possible participants, I identified African American adults between the ages of 20 and 40 with or without children in school. The study focused on people within this age range because African Americans in this age range attended school after the end of de jure segregation. During their time in K–12 education, they witnessed the advent of *A Nation At Risk*, national and state learning goals and standards, the increased focus on excellence as opposed to equity, the renaming of the "Black–White gap" (race focus) to the achievement gap (income focus), and the school accountability movement. In addition, those who have children have experience with the No Child Left Behind Act and high-stakes testing.

My goal was to identify between 10 and 15 participants. I did this by charting possible participants based on gender, age, educational attainment, career, current place of residence, and family of origin place of residence to obtain a heterogeneous group of participants. I selected 8 of 21 women and 7 of 9 men. The following is a list of the research participants.

- Kyle is an unmarried, 23-year-old male college student. He was raised by his mother in a low-income area in Chicago, where he attended public schools. Kyle experienced some academic struggles during his high school years. He recently completed an associate's degree from a local city college and, at the time of this research, attended a state university.

- Missy is an unmarried 40-year-old female. She was raised in Chicago, where she attended public schools. Missy is the mother of one son (age 6 at the time of this research). She has worked in public schools in a variety of capacities; however, she enrolled her son in a private school.
- Vanessa is an unmarried 20-year-old female college student. Vanessa attended public schools in Chicago. She was an average student who sometimes resented what she saw as a lack of opportunity in her high school. Vanessa decided to attend college after visiting a university attended by one of her close friends and seeing the variety of experiences offered in a college setting. At the time of this research, Vanessa was in her second year at a community college.
- Elizabeth is a married 34-year-old female. She grew up in a part of Chicago that she termed the "wild hundreds" with her parents and two siblings. She attended public schools and completed a bachelor's degree in communication. Elizabeth is the stepmother of two boys and the mother of one daughter (age 12 months at the time of this research).
- Georgette is a married 33-year-old female. She attended public schools in a small city in Illinois. Georgette's mother experienced a period of drug addiction while Georgette was growing up. Georgette combated the assumptions peers made about her life experiences. Georgette earned an associate's degree from a community college and now works in the health care field. At the time of this research, Georgette had assumed custody of her eight-year-old nephew (Darius). She is also mother of one son (age 15 months).
- Paulette is an unmarried 31-year-old female. She grew up in Chicago with her parents and a brother and sister. The family moved to a low-income area when Paulette was 12. She earned a bachelor's degree in sociology and, at the time of this research, was pursuing a master's degree.
- Rachel is an unmarried 38-year-old female who grew up in a suburban community in the New Orleans area. She attended predominantly White magnet schools for most of her years of schooling. Rachel was a high-achieving student who described herself as a "nerd." At the time of this research, she was living in Illinois and working toward an MBA.
- Janiece is a married 36-year-old female who grew up in a diverse city in Illinois. She was raised by her grandmother and great grandparents. Janiece completed a liberal arts degree and aspires to return to school to study criminal justice. At the time of this research, Janiece was the legal guardian of her two younger sisters (ages 18 and 14).
- Mena is an unmarried 32-year-old female who grew up in a predominantly White middle/upper-class community in Illinois. She attended public schools through eighth grade and then attended a private high school. Mena

completed a bachelor's degree in psychology and now works for a prominent parent-teacher organization. At the time of this research, Mena was completing a master's degree in training and development.

- Kevin is an engaged 34-year-old male who grew up in Louisiana with his parents and a sister and brother. His mother was a teacher. Kevin attended magnet schools and generally did well, although he did not participate in many of the clubs and activities that were available to him.
- Dudley is an unmarried 37-year-old male who grew up in Chicago. He was an only child, but he grew up with his parents and an extended family that included six cousins. Dudley attended public schools throughout elementary, middle, and high school. He received a bachelor's degree and at the time of this research lives in Illinois.
- Ralph is an unmarried 31-year-old male. He was raised by his parents, a teacher and an accountant-turned-plumber, in a small town in Mississippi. Ralph was a successful student, as was his younger sister. Ralph has a strong connection with schools because his mother, aunts, and uncles were all teachers. Ralph earned a master's degree in finance.
- Trig is an engaged 34-year-old male. He was raised by his parents in Chicago, where he attended public and parochial schools during his elementary school years. He attended a magnet high school. Trig was a member of a gang beginning in elementary school and continuing through young adulthood. He eventually earned a bachelor's degree and is planning to begin graduate work in his field. At the time of this research, Trig is the father of one son (age 18 months) and is planning his upcoming wedding.
- Daniel is an unmarried 24-year-old male who grew up in Chicago with his aunt, who raised him on a fixed income. Daniel attended public school and had marginal academic achievement. Daniel received training as an emergency medical technician. At the time of this research, Daniel was seeking employment.
- Mark is an unmarried 20-year-old male who grew up in Chicago with his extended family. Mark struggled through public school and considered dropping out of high school. He eventually graduated and enrolled at a city college where, at the time of this research, he was pursuing an associate's degree in a health care field.

I arranged to meet with each participant in a place that would be convenient for him/her. In all cases, we identified comfortable settings in which natural conversations could take place. In this way, I tried to minimize the sense of artificiality that often goes along with research. I interviewed one participant in her house, one at the local library, and the remainder at various local coffee shops. Two interviews were done in the morning or on a Saturday. The remainder of the interviews took place on weekday evenings after the participants left work or school for the day.

I conducted semi-structured ethnographic interviews focusing on the participant's beliefs about the education of African Americans and the achievement gap with a particular emphasis on their beliefs about ways to meet the needs of Black children. Ethnographic interviews are highly appropriate for research with African Americans. One reason for this, as discussed previously, is the African American cultural emphasis on narrative, personal experience, and dialogue (King, 2005). Unlike quantitative research methods that only describe the achievement gap and the factors that affect it, in-depth individual interviews can give us deeper insights into the cultural discourse on education and the achievement gap and have the added benefit of engaging African Americans in the important dialogue on how to effectively educate African American children (Vaughn et al. 1996).

When I started my research, I believed that in personal interviews with an African American researcher, African American participants would be more likely to share their experiences and provide their authentic reactions to questions. In addition, in this situation, African American participants would be more likely to speak in their comfortable, everyday language, choosing their words and intonations based on meaning as opposed to choosing their words to engineer how they sound. This would provide more trustworthy insight into the everyday discourse of African Americans on the subject. This everyday discourse represents the essence of Black culture and something that non-Blacks seldom if ever experience. As an "indigenous insider" (i.e., a researcher who is part of the culture and community being studied), I felt that I would benefit from all of these advantages (Tillman, 2006).

Even with this in mind, after conducting the interviews, I was surprised at the extent to which my status as a member of the African American community benefited me in my research. I found that each of the participants were extremely open and forthcoming throughout the interviews. They quickly relaxed and engaged in what I would characterize as a friendly conversation including a great deal of laughter. The participants shared stories about their experiences in schools as well as information about their families and meaningful events in their lives. Although I used specific interview questions with all participants, several participants spontaneously shared information and stories they felt related to education. One prefaced a very personal story by saying, "I can't believe I'm going to tell you this."

I was seeking to gain an understanding of all aspects of the educational discourse from the perspective of the participants in the absence of the lens of Whiteness. Unlike traditional research on the achievement gap and African American education, this study attempts to access the current educational discourse instead of seeking a justification for the outcome gap.

Analysis

Each interview was transcribed verbatim. I reviewed the transcripts along with my field notes and made note of the ideas that seemed to stand out to me at the time of the interviews. I used these ideas to begin the process of coding the transcripts based on themes and sub-themes. The interview data was analyzed using two primary methods. Using the transcripts of the interviews, I created a profile of each participant based on information gathered from a focused life history. In addition, I identified recurring themes within the interviews to gain some insight into themes in the educational discourse of the participants. I organized the themes based on their interrelationships and devised a metaphor or conceptual framework to describe the themes and demonstrate the interactions among them.

I used my cultural knowledge as part of the analysis and interpretation process and to supply what Tillman (2002) calls an "endarkened" perspective to inform theory and practice. I make no attempt to strive for objectivity. My analysis and interpretations are based on the anecdotes and information shared by the participants as well as my own personal experiences. The purpose of this study is not simply to tell a story or even to provide a counternarrative but to understand a perspective and to use that understanding as a researcher/practitioner/activist to affect educational change for African American children. To do this, I must present the results of a study in a way that maintains the cultural integrity of the participants and the larger community while also making the information accessible to educational practitioners and researchers (the vast majority of whom are outsiders to the African American community).

To strengthen the credibility of my conclusions and ensure cultural validity, each participant was given the opportunity to read his/her profile and the themes stemming from the interviews in order to provide feedback on the meaning of their stories and words. I also provided the participants with the conceptual framework for their review and input to ensure a culturally sensitive data interpretation (Tillman, 2002). Although I provided the entire work to the participants for review, I specifically encouraged their response to the framework that I use to describe their views. I received a few responses from participants. The feedback affirmed aspects of the analysis including the description of the roles of parents and teachers. I revised my discussion of the role of students based on participant feedback.

Although my aim in this research was to access a specific discourse, I was surprised by the extent to which the participants' stories, ideas, and beliefs displayed cohesiveness. The participants shared many similar comments about education and seemed to have similar analyses of their school experiences. Looking back on the interview experience, I was struck by the feeling or realization that there is indeed an African American culture. The extent to which this common culture was evident was surprising to me because of the diversity of the African American community. I found it comforting to face evidence of this common culture in the interviews. As an insider to the African American community, I experienced a feeling of connectedness both as I conversed with the participants and as I reviewed and analyzed the interview transcripts. This connectedness aided me in the process of analysis.

The following chapter shares the results of my discussions with the participants. The achievement gap ideology and the outcome gap are intertwined in the experiences of African American community members as they relate to education. In Chapter 4, based on the participants' stories and comments, anecdotal evidence, history, and personal experience, I present a conceptual framework in the form of a metaphor that helps us to explore African American community members' beliefs about education. I use the framework to explore the African American community members' views of the roles of parents, teachers, and students and their analysis of the achievement gap.

I began this work by reminding the reader that if we want our rhetoric to match our reality, we must open a dialogue about what African American children need. This dialogue must take place on equal terms. I invite the reader to engage in an uncommon exercise of examining one's own beliefs and considering how those beliefs affect the lives of others. I ask educators, administrators, and policymakers to suspend their disbelief and consider what children, families, and communities with a distinct culture, belief system, history, and experiences might want, need and deserve from schools.

Chapter 4

The Purposeful Educational Transaction

"History does not furnish a case of the elevation of a people by ignoring the thought and aspiration of the people thus served."

—Woodson, 1933, p 24

This is a story about 15 African American community members' views of education. I argue that for these African American community members, education is a purposeful transaction between the teacher and the student that is mediated by the parent and that this view coincides with the views and discourse of historical African American thinkers (see Figure 4.1). I present a conceptual framework aimed at helping the reader understand the patterns of thoughts, beliefs, and stories shared in this discourse.

This chapter is divided into three main sections. First, I explain the metaphor of education as a purposeful transaction and its connection to historical African American thought. In the next section, I share the roles and responsibilities inherent in the educational transaction. This section includes a discussion of the roles of parents, teachers, and students as shared by the participants. In the section titled "Conducting the Transaction," I examine the interaction among the roles of parents, teachers, and students as identified by the participants. This includes a discussion of the participants' analyses of the outcome gap in terms of the purposeful transaction framework.

EDUCATION AS A TRANSACTION

The view of education shared by the 15 African American community members can be viewed as a purposeful educational transaction. The term "transaction" reflects that the purpose of education in African American culture is

51

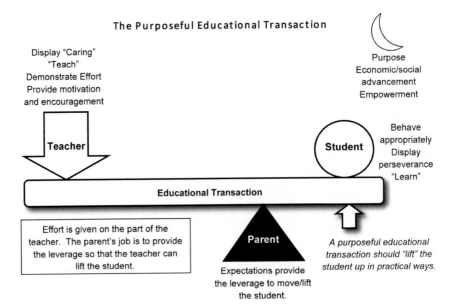

Figure 4.1

inexorably connected to individual and collective economics, empowerment, and social capital. A transaction is defined as an "instance of doing business," "the act of negotiating something or carrying out a business deal," and "a communication or activity between two or more people that influences and affects all of them" (Encarta, 2007). The African American cultural ideal of education coincides with each of these definitions. The purposeful educational transaction is a conceptual framework that provides a way of understanding these African American community members' views of the roles, responsibilities, purpose, and process of education.

Education is a "good" that is conferred upon the recipient through a service. The essence of the educational transaction is a give-and-take process in which the teacher imparts knowledge, information, and skills to the student, who must collect and store the knowledge and information and demonstrate the skills on demand. The student pays for this service through appropriate behavior, effort and personal growth. The educational transaction involves relationships and roles that are negotiated primarily by the parent.

In this transaction, the teacher has both the responsibility of a servant and the authority of a merchant. The student acts essentially as a consumer, while the parent oversees the transaction. This viewpoint reflects African American educational thought throughout history in the United States.

A transaction is only negotiated for a good or service that has discernible value. Frederick Douglass' childhood story of trading bread for reading lessons from a destitute White child provides an example of trading for the good and service of education. Inherent in this kind of transaction is the belief on the part of the consumer that the practical value of the goods and services being received warrants the price to be paid. Ogbu (2001) argued that African Americans as involuntary immigrants do not see a predictable connection between schooling and success. As a result, African American youth conceive of themselves in opposition to what they conceive as "acting White."

However, historic African American educational thought suggests the opposite, with the discourse placing an intensely high value on education as a source of empowerment. W. E. B. Du Bois and Booker T. Washington each advanced this idea as they advocated for education as a way to produce economic, social, and political advancement for the race. The effective education of the individual was promoted as the way to change the circumstances of the collective.

Du Bois' concept of the "Talented Tenth" exemplifies this way of thinking. He argued that by identifying the most talented 10 percent of the Black population and providing them with the best liberal education, the nation could provide effective leaders to uplift the African American community. Washington argued for a different kind of education to achieve the same end. His promotion of vocational education for the individual supported the ideals of hard work, thrift, and patience as a way to achieve the collective goals of the African American community. These ideas continue to resonate within the African American community.

For example, this research was supported by a group of participants who believed in assisting the individual to help the collective. Upon receiving a call or e-mail from a fellow African American community member about a Black woman who needed to conduct interviews to complete her doctorate, numerous individuals volunteered to give some of their time to help a "sister" complete her education. (Several participants' use of the term "sister" to refer to me reflects their recognition of my status as an indigenous insider of the African American community.) Some reflected on the fact that they would like to continue their education someday. Others shared about the encouragement and support they received in pursuing their current level of education. Their support was based on the idea of a collective responsibility for the uplift of the African American community. By helping an individual they see as a "sister," they in turn contribute to the community.

Trig, a systems analyst who teaches computer classes for children on the weekend, remembered his father setting an example of giving back.

I think that there's too much danger in making articulate, educated people who don't understand responsibility as a part of the world. For instance, my father volunteered for junior achievement, and there would be times that I would wanna do things and I couldn't understand why he was so committed to the other kids. And then I realized that he understood that he had a greater role in society. I think education too often focuses on the individual learner, rather than the learning community as a whole.

The central purpose of the educational transaction is to lift the student from his/her current condition and status to a state of economic and social empowerment that strengthens the individual, family, and community. To this end, African Americans view education pragmatically. Schooling should prepare young people in practical ways. Carter G. Woodson (1933) noted that education is "the most important thing in the uplift of the Negro." In his view, the prevalent system of educating African American youth was actually responsible for "miseducating" members of the Black community.

One component of miseducation was ignoring a practical education that could help young Black people make a living and improve their circumstances by making use of their personal, family, and community resources. "If the 'highly educated' Negro would forget most of the untried theories taught him in school, if he could see through the propaganda which has been instilled into his mind under the pretext of education, if he would fall in love with his own people and begin to sacrifice for their uplift—if the 'highly educated' Negro would do these things, he could solve some of the problems now confronting the race" (Woodson, 1993, p 44).

The idea that education is pursued for economic and social uplift continues to be an important theme in the participants' discourse on education. Education is about having opportunities, getting the things you want, taking care of yourself, having something that no one can take away, and making life better for one's family. The educational transaction has a clear, pragmatic purpose. It is not focused on pursuing education for its own sake.

Ralph's father left a job at a large corporation to open his own plumbing business. He was successful at maintaining a business with which he could support his family. Still, when Ralph began learning about the business, his father advised him to "work with your mind, not with your back." He wanted Ralph to get the education necessary to allow him to choose how he would make a living.

For Ralph, the pursuit of a college degree was the way to take his father's advice. He commented,

College prepared me for a lot. . . . It was very important. I think education gives you a key to a door, and what you do when you walk into that door is kind of up to you, but it gives you the background so you can actually walk through the door and be able to get into that group of people that you're trying to fit in with. People who do it every day may be more knowledgeable than you, but you at least have the basic concepts, and that's the whole point.

If you get that point, you can grow to the point where you move up the ladder, but you just want to stay in the room. It all prepared me in different ways. All of them worked together to get me to the point where I am. Without them, I wouldn't even sit here. You'd be interviewing somebody else that had a little bit more education and background.

My conversation with Mena exemplifies the sense of purpose inherent in the purposeful educational transaction. Mena was a 32-year-old training and development specialist for a national organization. Now living in Chicago, Mena grew up in a small, predominantly White community in Illinois. As a teenager, she sometimes frustrated her mother because of her nonchalant attitude about grades, but, over time, Mena embraced the belief in the power of education. Mena's pursuit of education is a major value in her life.

> [Education] was your ticket, and it was very well known—very much known and pushed in our house that that's the key. That is your way to get different levels and layers. [It was] something that even once I had received my bachelor's degree, it was resonating for me. . . . Even to this day, I see [education] as my way of getting in, and getting up, moving on to the next level, as far as my professional career goes and my life.

In some ways Booker T. Washington and W. E. B. Du Bois represented opposing viewpoints on how to elevate African Americans to full social, economic, and political equality. However, they each promoted education as a prerequisite for improved circumstances. Their logic continues to be used by African Americans in communicating the importance of education.

Although the educational transaction is meant to change an individual's circumstances, it does not change an individual's personal worth, status within the African American community, or identity. Education that causes the student to lose his sense of self and his understanding of his role within the family and community is miseducation. This kind of education begins with what Woodson calls the "propaganda" of Black inferiority.

He noted that most educated Blacks became so in an atmosphere that taught them that they were inferior and that success was impossible for the Black community. "To handicap a student by teaching him that his black face is a curse and that his struggle to change his condition is hopeless is the worst sort of lynching" (Woodson, 1933, p. 3). This process of "handicapping" Black students may be the source of what Ogbu and others have identified as African American students' aversion to "acting White."

Kyle struggled off and on as he worked his way through school. Living in poverty as the child of a single mother, he faced the low expectations and opposition of teachers who were annoyed by his insistence on participating in advanced programs and school activities. The propaganda Kyle faced was overt.

> I would always come home and feel bad, crying, because, you know, my teachers would talk down to me and tell me I wouldn't be anything and that I would be selling drugs and hanging out in the parks, sleeping on benches or whatever. [My mother would] always tell me, "you can do it, I don't care what they say."
>
> I mean, if you [teachers] feel that I'm not good enough and I'm constantly being told that I'm not good enough and I can't accomplish anything in life because of my circumstances, then pretty much sooner or later that's going to start taking affect on me psychologically. And as a result of that a lot of kids don't finish school because they don't feel comfortable there. They don't feel welcomed. You know, I'm constantly being told that I'm not good enough, I'm dumb, or I'm this or I'm that, and you know, you get tired of hearing it. So they stop going to school, which is very bad, and it is very detrimental to their lives.
>
> But, I mean, at the same time, you can kind of understand. I mean, you know, nobody's going to come around a place where they're constantly being ridiculed, or scorned, or mistreated. So, you know, [society's] whole persona about African American students is going to definitely have to change.

African American youth continue to face the propaganda of inferiority and hopelessness as they are exposed to the achievement gap ideology. As a high school student, I entered my sophomore level English class to be greeted by the teacher standing by the board. When all of the students were seated, she wrote the following words on the board: "1 out of every 4 Black males will go to prison before the age of 24." That quote stayed on the board for the rest of the class.

I am sure the teacher's intentions were well-meaning in sharing this statistic with the class. My guess is that this information had been shared with her and she wanted to use this statistic to motivate students to work hard to achieve. However, her intentions were lost on me and my classmates. I remember seething with anger and some embarrassment as one of only two African Americans in the class. It seemed like a personal affront to me and other African Americans to promote that statistic. Whether intentional or unintentional, the communication of the idea that failure is probable or inevitable exacerbates the achievement gap ideology.

As an eighth grader, Kyle achieved one of the highest scores on the placement test for high school. However, when one student who was unhappy with her score went to the school administration to complain about the test, the administrators decided to insist that all students retake the test. It was stated that some students received a higher score than was expected and that this suggested some cheating may have taken place. Kyle was one of the students who were pointed out as receiving a higher score than expected. He and all of the other eighth grade students in the school were forced to retake the test. Because the teachers and administrators held low expectations for Kyle's achievement, his strong performance was startling. Kyle's perceived over-achievement brought suspicion instead of celebration and encouragement.

> When she did that, I mean, it really did something to me because, you know, it's like an insult. It's like slap in the face. Okay, well, I couldn't have scored as high because, you know, I had someone helping me out. You know, which was totally—and it wasn't true and it was really insulting.

Kyle took the test a second time and once again received a near-perfect score.

The achievement gap ideology also affects the way teachers respond to student needs. As a district administrator in a medium-sized pre-K–12 school district in Illinois, one of my jobs is to monitor, promote, and improve student achievement for all students at every grade level. Over the past several years one of the district's schools had an inordinately large outcome gap between African American students and White students in all subject areas. When the district administrators met with the school administration and an influential group of teacher leaders to discuss reasons for the gap and ways to address it, a highly educated, veteran teacher summed up what he saw as the problem: "The Black kids don't want to do well. They talk about it out in the hallways, and they're *loud*" (emphasis added).

The 15 African American community members described the achievement gap ideology in two main ways. Educators and policymakers were either seen as having low expectations for African American students and little or no concern for their achievement or they were seen as expecting little from the students and treating them as though they were incapable of academic success. These viewpoints reflect the conservative and liberal traditional views of the achievement gap ideology. Rachel described herself as a nerd when going through school. Rachel's words for educational policymakers advise against pitying African American youth.

> I think that they don't have to treat African-American children as if they're handicapped because I still think that's what they think—that we need to be babied, but really we don't. What we need is access to the same materials, same

information, the same programs that our counterparts have in school, but if we have the same—I'm not saying like separate but equal. If we still have—if we have the same material or access to the same libraries, the same books, computer programs and stuff like that, then we will learn it. I think right now it's just a matter of we don't have access to exactly the same things that a lot of our counterparts do. And they tend to handicap us and say, "Oh, poor babies, poor babies. They're not learning." No, just give us what we need to learn. Give us what we need, and we will be fine.

Ralph explained what he sees as a differential investment in African American students based on perceived probability of success.

School curriculum is not influenced by the African American community. It's influenced by individuals who have greater opportunities than the general African American student. . . . Most African American students I know, families I know don't take their kids to Sylvan Learning Center or they don't take their kids to places like other learning centers and other programs like that because they can't afford it. I've only known two people in my entire life that have been taught by Sylvan Learning Center. The school system assumes that the parent at home is working with the student, and in a lot of African American families, that doesn't happen because the parents are working and don't have time.

From the school system perspective, they don't cater to the African American students. They cater to the percentage of students that they feel are going to succeed.

The communication of low expectations in schools, in the media, and in the community is detrimental to all African American youth including those who are performing well.

As are result of being steeped in the achievement gap ideology throughout their years of schooling, educated African Americans sometimes focus their efforts on changing their identity to imitate Whites. African American discourse fervently warns youth against forgetting from whence they come and forsaking the African American community and its institutions. In a September 2007 interview hosted by African American talk show host Tavis Smiley, Dr. Cornel West referred to this phenomenon. Tavis Smiley asked about well-educated African Americans returning to their home communities. Dr. West immediately picked up the reference. In his words, "They used to say on the block that Harvard has ruined more Negroes than bad whiskey and there's something to that. You get up there and get Harvarditis and Yaleitis, Princetonitis, or whatever. Stanforditis" (West, 2007).

Dr. West went on to describe the ways that Ivy League-educated African Americans sometimes look down on the Black community and reject the wisdom of their elders. While African American community members value the educational transaction and take pride in the accomplishments of youth who realize the purpose of education, African American culture does not view education as something that should change an individual's view of their status in the family or community.

ROLES AND RESPONSIBILITIES IN THE TRANSACTION

The purposeful educational transaction takes the form of a lever that is designed to move or lift the student toward empowerment. The success of the educational transaction rests on the roles played by the student, the teacher, and the parent. In this conceptual framework, the teacher applies the effort or force necessary to lift the student. The student places all focus on achieving the purpose of education. The role of the parent is pivotal to the success of the transaction because the parent serves as the fulcrum that makes leverage possible.

The Parent's Role: Expectation Setting

The parent's role is to set and communicate expectations for the student and the teacher. The importance of the parent's role in helping young people navigate through society is common in all cultures, but guiding youth through the expression of high expectations for perseverance, independence, and success in the face of struggle and opposition is a significant theme in the African American discourse. James Baldwin expressed the passionate expression of love and expectation for his nephew, "I know how black it looks today for you. It looked bad that day, too, yes, we were trembling. We have not stopped trembling yet, but if we had not loved each other none of us would have survived. And now you must survive because we love you, and for the sake of your children and your children's children" (1962, p. 7).

One of the ways the participants communicated their expectations for students is by sharing personal, family, and historical stories of struggle, perseverance, and overcoming. The teaching of African American history plays an important role in this process. When it is not taught by schools, families fill the void by discussing African American historical figures and achievements at home and in the community. These stories function like morality plays designed to teach youth to persevere in the face of opposition.

Mena spoke about the generational emphasis on education in her family starting with her family's quest to escape the sharecropping system of the South. Mena's mother shared stories of their history to explain her focus on education.

There was always strong push for my mother, as there was from her grandparents who raised her. She grew up during a time where the South was still segregated, and during her high school and junior high school years, they then—segregation was over, and they allowed them back into the school, so it was always a really big push, with them being sharecroppers and wanting a better life for their grandchildren, to be educated and to get an education, and that was your way out, and her way out of the segregated South, and being a sharecropper, and living that whole life. Because that was what she was raised with, and that was her story, and that actually had helped her to become successful, that was a very big push.

For generations in Mena's family, obtaining an education was the key to obtaining autonomy and economic freedom.

African American parents communicate the expectation that young people demonstrate independence as they navigate through situations in school and society. The student bears a high level of responsibility for his/her own success or failure. The participants' parents made the expectations clear. "Get an education. Get your own. Take care of yourself. The rest can wait." This was the frequent refrain of Elizabeth's mother. Elizabeth followed this advice better than all of her siblings, but she remembered that is was not always easy.

I remember being at the dining room table just crying, "I don't understand this stuff." And [my mother] didn't remember it either by the time I got to it, so she's like, "Baby, just do the best you can." And she would stand there all night, too, until I figured it out.

Elizabeth's mother stayed up with Elizabeth as she struggled with her homework, although she could not help with the actual work. Elizabeth's mother's presence was both an encouragement and a method of ensuring accountability.

The participants' parents support the educational transaction by holding the student accountable for appropriate behavior, effort, independence, and perseverance and by holding the teacher accountable for "caring," exhibiting effort, motivating the student, and "teaching." To do this, the parents maintained a relationship with both the student and the teacher. This was done by monitoring the educational transaction and stepping in to correct or mediate problems that were perceived. Parents also assumed responsibility for protecting the student from what was perceived to be unjust or harsh treatment by the teacher or school.

Kevin, the father of a two-year-old son, shared his expectations for his children and himself.

Number one, I really want to teach them to respect their teachers, respect their elders. Even if you think, I'm not going to tell them this in the beginning, but, you know, even if you think that the person doesn't have your best interest, you have to respect them regardless. And later on that's when I come in and I can see what is going on . . . if I feel like it's fair or not. Because I'm going to know what is happening and going on. I'm going to ask you everyday what's going on.

Mena's mother stepped in to mediate her relationship with her teacher after a disappointing parent teacher conference:

Mena: When I was in third or fourth grade, my teacher wanted to put me in the telephone booth closet the whole day—there by myself because she felt like I was disrupting class or I was talking too much to my other peers. . . . That was the way to address the issue instead of taking alternate routes. That was her way of trying to deal with that and me—was let's get her, separate her, isolate her in this closet, and she will be in there all day. This closet had no windows, just this—it was literally a cement closet that they would take private phone calls in.

I remember my mother coming back from the parent-teacher conference and that being the statement, and her being humiliated by that, but then she was also upset that [the teacher] wanted to put me in this closet, and [my mother] tried to reprimand me for that, like bad behavior, but at the same time [she was] like, "Seriously? You wanna put my daughter in a closet?" and a little upset that I had pushed this woman to the point where she felt that need, but then . . . [the teacher] didn't know necessarily how to deal with an African American young girl who just talked too much.

That was her way of addressing that, instead of taking an alternate route—that wasn't an option for other students, their parents, but yeah, for her, she wanted to throw me away in this closet. I think it was seeing it from the side, as an adult, like "Hey, wait a minute. Would you suggest that to other parents, or is it just my kid?" but also being a little upset because that's something you don't want as a parent—you don't want your child's teacher to have to say about that them in the parent-teacher conference.

Interviewer: Okay. So what came of that? I take it that you never got moved to the closet.

Mena: I never went in the closet. Needless to say, I think I got a little belt action, maybe, or grounded. I can't remember exactly what, but I didn't go in the closet, but then it wasn't a problem. I remember that it was definitely solved that evening, and from that point out, obviously, yeah, I didn't go in the closet.

Mena later learned that her mother also had a private conversation with the teacher—who never made the suggestion again.

Georgette's mother also stepped in to protect her from perceived bias.

I had one math teacher, and I can't remember her name. It'll come to me, I'm sure. She just, for some reason, had an attitude when it came to me. And so I would finish my math work and then pull out something else to do so I wouldn't have homework today. And she would say, "That's not math. You can't do that." And I was like, "Okay. Well, I'm done with the stuff that you gave us." So finally, she just—if I was late to class, the pass I had wasn't good enough, or whatever the case may be. I had an A in her class, and then I went to my dean, who was like a second mom to me, and I was like, "Something's wrong with her."

So I told my mom about it, and then my mom called this conference. And the conference lasted about five or ten minutes, and my mom met with her and my mom was like, "As far as I know, Georgette has an A in your class and she's not disruptive. I don't want to ever hear her come home again telling me about anything that you're doing, or else I'm gonna go above Miss Smith's head and above Dr. Simpson's head," that's what mom told her. So that was the end of that meeting, and I didn't have any problems with her after that.

The expectation for parents to play their role of upholding high expectations and monitoring the educational transaction is a strongly held value. The African American community members communicated this expectation to one another and express disdain for those who fail to uphold their role in the transaction. Missy, the mother of a six-year-old son, whom she enrolled in private school, assigned the burden of monitoring student learning to parents as part of their expectation setting responsibilities.

If you're a parent, you know that your child can't read, or is having difficulty reading. Then, it's your responsibility to go to the teacher and say, "Well, I listened to little Johnny read the other night, and he was having some problems. What are you doing to—what's his curriculum like, to kind of help?"

It goes back to the parent, and then, to the teacher. If I knew my son was having a problem, I help him, but then, I'm also on the phone talking to his teacher, saying, "That homework he had last night, he had a little difficulty. Are you going over this before giving the homework? What are you doing?" Responsibility lies with the parent, and then, with the teacher.

Kevin expressed the expectations for parents when he described how he would work with his own child.

I might not come to every parent/teacher conference, or I might be busy and my wife may go. I might not be at every program, but I'm going to be to as many as

I can. But I guarantee you I'm going to know what's going on in the classroom with you because I'm going to ask you every day at home. And it ain't going to be "ah, it's fine." No, it ain't fine, what did you do? So I'm just going to try and instill that in them early. You know, I guess to just encourage them and guide them even if you're not doing well. Because if you don't have that dialog, you don't know where to start with your kid and where to improve.

Like, you know, what do you need help with, son? You know, do you know how to study? I would just encourage that dialog and communication and what's going on when they get old enough. You know, well, I didn't do well. Well, son why didn't you do well? What do you need?

Well, I didn't do well in this subject. We didn't think about consequences. Well, I'm just trying to do it this way. Well, why don't you try it this way? This way might work for you. You know, I read slow. So it has taken me awhile to figure something out. I have to read it, you read it, write it down, highlight it, and read it again. Well, someone read it the first time and they stand up there and they're done with it. They have to realize you can't compare yourself with student B, you have to do what you do best and not what they do best. So I'm going to try to encourage that to all them. That's one thing I want to do.

Neither student expectations nor parent support for the educational transaction involves the "work" of teaching. This work is reserved for the teacher. In fact, the belief that "teaching" academic skills is the exclusive role of the teacher is so strong that the African American community members expressed indignation and resentment about having this responsibility placed on their shoulders.

When Missy's son experienced some problems in first grade, she questioned the teacher's willingness to teach.

I'd get calls that he wasn't doing well in school. And I—they know me up at school. I don't think she wanted to teach first grade—and it showed. It showed in the fact that she let the students, kind of, do what they wanted to do. If the student—if he put his head down, she would allow that. And I had an issue with that. And I told her, "I'm not paying $3,000 in tuition for you to let him lay his head down. What are you doing to motivate him? You have him for eight hours a day. What are you doing? I'm doing my part by helping with his homework, giving him supplies, giving him encouragement, but what are you doing to make it interesting?" He loved kindergarten. His kindergarten teacher made it interesting.

"What are you doing?" And she couldn't give me an answer because I don't think she wanted to teach it, and it showed.

The Educator's Role: "Teach"ing in the Transaction

Within the African American conceptual framework of education shared by the participants, the word "teach" denotes specific activities. To teach means to impart knowledge to a student through direct means. A teacher is expected to be an expert who provides knowledge to the student. Although students are not seen as blank slates to be shaped by the teacher, both parents and students expect the teacher to impart knowledge and skills by a process of show and tell. The skills taught by the teacher are necessary to promote the student's independence. The teacher is expected to be the authority, the leader, and the presenter in the classroom. This way of thinking may not recognize the idea of teacher as facilitator as "teaching" especially if the teacher does not exhibit personal authority.

By high school, Dudley had a well-defined idea of what teachers should do. His idea often conflicted with those of his teachers, particularly when it came to math instruction.

> The teacher had put up a formula on the board, and she said, "Okay. Go up there and solve it for me."
>
> I go up there and solve the formula and she asked me, "Okay. Well, how did you do it?"
>
> "I don't know."
>
> She was like "Well, how you know it's right?"
>
> "Cause that's the right answer. You can trace back through it all you want."
>
> I didn't know how it was, how I did it. But X equaled something at the end, and that was right, and that's all I knew. She wanted me to explain it. I was like "Look. I got up there and worked the problem out. You're the teacher. You explain it."

The teacher's role in the educational transaction is paramount. The participants' belief in and embrace of authority result in high expectations and a high level of respect for the role of the teacher. It also means that teachers are those most responsible for doing the "work" necessary to make the educational transaction effective. African American discourse places a high value on authority. In the African American culture, respect is reserved for those who gain and exhibit authority through their personal characteristics and actions. Teachers who possess this kind of personal authority contribute a great deal of power to the educational transaction.

Georgette explained one rationale for trusting teachers with the work of educating students.

> I just want to make sure that you [the teacher] know what's going on because you're with him for like eight hours a day, and I'm not there. So you're really his parent during that time. I'm teaching him that he has to listen to you and respect you and do what you tell him to do, so I'm gonna assume that you're guiding him in the right direction. In order to do that, you need to know what's going

on. You need to know that if he comes to school saying, "My life sucks," well, why he's saying it. You need to know all the faces of Darius, and everything that he's been through, or if he woke up on the wrong side of the bed.

The high expectations held for teachers in the African American culture are evident in the works of African American leaders. Woodson (1933) argued that African American schools had few teachers who knew "about the children whom they teach or about their parents who influence the pupils more than the teachers themselves" (p. 145). He addressed the question of whether it was right to place the burden on teachers to change the society. His response exemplifies the view of teachers in the educational transaction. "But can you expect teachers to revolutionize the social order for the good of the community? Indeed we must expect this very thing. The educational system of a country is worthless unless it accomplishes this task" (Woodson, 1933, p.145).

The educational transaction takes place between individuals with the school as the backdrop for the transaction. For African Americans, the central purpose of the educational system is to provide the resources and support necessary for the teacher to uplift the students. Siddle-Walker's studies of African American teachers of segregated schools in the South supports the idea of the reverence and responsibility placed in the role of the teacher (2002).

She found that many Black teachers in segregated school systems were highly credentialed. They saw their role as one of preparing students to not only make a living but also to successfully negotiate a society that saw them as inferior. Teachers were integral and well-respected members of the Black community. They accepted the responsibility of being the experts on teaching, providing direct instruction, echoing the values of the community, maintaining relationships with parents as fellow community members, and creating a disciplined and empowering school environment.

Teachers provide the force of the educational transaction by "teaching," displaying caring, providing motivation and encouragement, and by establishing and maintaining a relationship of trust with both the student and the parent. At best, the teacher has extraordinary power to make a transaction take place that is transformational for the student. This takes place when an individual teacher engages in the transaction by working and going the extra mile to support a student's achievement of the purpose of education.

For example, Mena attended high school on the south side of Chicago. It was her responsibility to get to and from school on the city bus and navigate through the numerous dangers within the community. Similar to the teachers described in Siddle-Walker's work, when Mena arrived at school, her teachers did the work necessary to ensure her success.

My science teacher, Mr. Williams, fabulous man. I have a lot of teachers in my past that I felt like were almost surrogate parents and that mattered a lot to me, too, because sometimes I just think back and I'm like, man, I wonder if I would have turned out the same or had the same kind of results if I didn't have these people that I saw every day that were encouraging me to be the best that I can be or encouraging me. One year when I wanted to be a teacher, he would get me information on being a teacher or I was really interested in science and he was a science teacher, so of course, he was all thrilled about that.

He would come to work early in the morning and have me meet him there, help me with science projects, you know, getting me into the science fairs, helping me purchase things for my project. I believe he even drove me to—like after you make it from the science fair at the school, you go to district and it would be at a community college. I can't remember the name of it. I think it was Olive Harvey or something like that. And I remember one particular year he drove me up there so that I could go. You know, my mom didn't have a car. He drove me up there, dropped me off, went to school, worked, came back and picked me up after everything was over. I will never forget that.

Part of the participants' expectation of a teacher is a commitment to the success of the student as an individual. Students can be successful when they see that commitment from teachers year after year. This is important because each school year brings about a new transaction between the student and a new teacher. Mena was fortunate to have a series of outstanding teachers.

It was him; it was another teacher, Ms. Magnivite. That was my eighth grade teacher and by the time I got to her, I was really into writing. So she had all types of stuff . . . for the computer in the classroom. What was the name of that game? *Oregon Trail*, we would play that a lot. She let me play that and just really encourage me to sharpen my writing skills, would enter me in book writing contests, essay contests. And I think it was at least one teacher that I remember every couple of years that kind of—it was like a handoff, you know.

And it started second in kindergarten. I remember her, Ms. Davis. I don't believe I was really into anything, but I just remember her being so happy to see me all the time and, "Oh, my God," just making a really big deal. And that makes a kid happy, you know, someone that's open armed to them all the time.

I really believed it was those relationships that I developed with those teachers that really encouraged me to endure the fights on the bus, the teasing because I had on a Morgan Park jacket. And then later on—and things inside the school got to a point where you were just glad it was time to graduate. And the girls started fighting more than the boys and it wasn't just fist fighting now. No, they're bringing razorblades to school, somebody has a gun off-campus, you know. I actually saw the progression and its just mind blowing.

But I really can't think of any other factor that really made me feel like at the time that it was worth it. They took their subjects and created such an environment in the classroom where you forgot about all that stuff until it was time to go through it again. But then you're like, "Okay, but we're doing the next part." Or it's my turn to read today, or it's my turn to present my project today, so definitely the encouragement, I would say, from the teachers and my experiences with them helped me deal with everything else.

Even when the students did not feel positively about the teacher's personal characteristics, they valued the teacher's level of caring and willingness to challenge them. They also valued teachers who embraced a positive relationship with their parents even though this often meant that they "couldn't get away with anything." Ralph grew up in an education family. His aunts and uncles were teachers and his mother was an administrator, so his family was known in the community. He recalled the way his teachers and family members would work together to hold him accountable. "I got a demerit at school once. My mom knew about it before I got off the bus." The communication between teachers and parents supported the parent's role in holding the student accountable. The students came to value that as they grew up.

Paulette provided another example of valuing a teacher's willingness to challenge a student.

One particular, Mr. N in high school, ironically, during the time, we knew we had this very pull and tug kind of relationship, very adversarial during that time, struggling to get—him trying to get the best out of me and make me achieve, and me being upset because he's not understanding my point of view, and I thought this was a subjective paper—very much of a struggle, and him calling me on just reading the Cliff notes and not the full book.

During the time, I didn't care for him very much, but I remember when I took placement tests to get into college, for first year, where they have to place you in English and math, and we had to write a paper. I believe it was on an experience that you remember as a child. I remember I wrote a short story about my first experience in a spelling bee and misspelling the word "furniture," and how that made me feel, how embarrassed I was, and my mom actually took off work to come here. My god, how could I not know that there was an "i" in furniture? I wrote this little story about that, and I remember when I met with my counselor afterwards.

I remember speaking to my counselor and advisors about taking the placement test [for] English and math, and she was looking at the computer screen. [She] didn't even bother to look up at me and say, "Hi. How're you doing?" when I walked into her office, but when my scores came up and she saw my English score, she turned back around to look at me as though she needed to see who this person was, that scored that high on the English portion. She just gave me this look like, "Really?" I'm like, "Yeah," and I'm sure she got the contrast, too, with the math score, and was probably like okay, this is really crazy.

So that was one of the things I remember—going back and thanking Mr. N my freshman year of college for participating and helping me pull through, and noticing, and seeing something in me that I guess I didn't see in myself.

At worst, teachers have the power to ensure that the transaction does not take place. This is done by failing to apply their effort/force in the right direction. When Kyle entered high school he was enrolled in the school's International Baccalaureate program. The program provided academically talented students with high-level instruction that would eventually allow them to earn college credits in high school. Kyle struggled with the first math class and approached the teacher for help.

I had a serious problem with Ms. Hudson because, you know, as I stated before I was in the International Baccalaureate Program when I first got in high school, and she was one of the top math teachers in the school, so all the Baccalaureate students took her math class. I can remember several times I went to her and asked her to, you know, kind of explain the problems a little bit more, I was having a comprehension problem with it, and she just didn't care.

She was like, "Well, it's not really my problem, you know. How did you get into this program? This is for kids who are above level, and you can't do the work. I shouldn't have to explain anything to you. You should already know how to do it." And I mean, if you're a high school student in your freshman year, I mean, you know, this just does something to you, you know.

The teacher's assertion that "I shouldn't have to explain anything to you; you should already know it" is diametrically opposed to the role of the teacher in the purposeful educational transaction.

Regardless of their intentions, teachers who do not show strong effort to ensure student success communicate a lack of caring to African American students. Similar to their parents, the participants evaluated their teachers based on their level of caring as demonstrated through efforts to motivate, provide assistance, and ensure success. Paulette's voice expressed frustration and outrage as she described her least favorite teacher.

Well, I'd have to say that teacher was my high school geometry teacher. She was very lazy. She was extremely lazy. And when I say that, I say that because you have your geometry books, and say we're learning something about degrees of angles. We're learning 30, 60, 90, 40 degree angles, whatever. The reflectives, symmetric, or—I'm just going off pure memory here—things like that.

She'd just open the book up, and she say, "Look on page 24, and look at the different examples of reflective versus symmetric versus," whatever other kind of angles there are or whatever. And she would be like, "And just read page 24, and let me know if you have any questions."

She did not help anybody when she was there. She'd sit behind her desk. She'd look mean the whole, entire time. She'd read a *People* magazine. I remember it so vividly. And she always wore—it just seemed she always wore this red skirt everyday.

She didn't care. She didn't care. She didn't care! And she'd say—when there was a test, she'd say, "It's a open-book test." It better be open-book, and you ain't teach nothing. So anyway. . . . I know [geometry] from the book. So I did not do well in that class, and I did not like that teacher.

The Student's Role: "Learn"ing in the Transaction

The role played by students in the educational transaction model may appear to be passive with the student as the consumer of the transaction who benefits from the work of the teacher and support of the parent. However, the effort and characteristics of students that are considered ideal by the African American community are worth further examination.

Actions that may be seen as misbehavior in schools are sometimes promoted by parents because they demonstrate independence and a willingness to fight (figuratively and literally) to navigate the social environment. As a child, Elizabeth was surprised when her mother "got tough" and told her she had to learn to fight back after she was in a fight at school.

So I was like, "You ain't bad," so I pushed her or whatever. And then, that's when the fight started. So Julie scratched my face, like, it was a real bad scratch like a—almost like a Nike sign. It was three scratches, and it was really deep scratches. So I run home, and I'm crying, and I'm telling my momma what happened—this, that, and the other. She can't believe that the girl had scratched my face up like that. So my momma, surprisingly, got tough with me and told me that, "You gonna have to learn how to fight. You can't keep running from these kids. You gonna have to learn how to defend yourself. Look at your face."

African American youth are often raised within a discourse of struggle. The ability to overcome, struggle through adversity, and succeed in spite of societal conditions is a predominant idea in African American culture. The ideals in the song "We Shall Overcome" are also seen in the interaction with teachers and school systems. It is part of the expectations held by parents and the role played by students.

When the teacher is seen as a damaging force to be overcome the ideal of the student as an overcomer can cause conflict. This was the case when Ralph was enrolled in the eighth grade biology class. Ralph, who was a bright student with a particular strength in science, spent a significant amount of time reading comic books in biology class. When confronted about this behavior, he told the teacher that he already understood the material and that it was "ridiculous" to work on the same concept for five days. When it came time for the teacher to recommend that next course to take, the teacher told Ralph that he would not be successful in chemistry or physics because these were rigorous courses and he did not have the attention span needed to do well. Ralph went home and told his mother about the conversation.

> My mom basically went ballistic, but she didn't say anything. I was very calm about it for some reason. I said, "Okay, fine. Whatever." I went ahead and took it and got an A. I took both of my report cards for the next two years and I took them right back to her class and said thank you for motivating me. I just wanted to let you know that I had the attention span to do these. I wrote that at the bottom. The principal wasn't too happy about that. He said that wasn't necessary. I said I just wanted to let her know that I remembered what she said.

Rachel planned to remind her children of their role as overcomers. When asked what she would tell her children about education, she replied,

> Get as much of it as you can, and don't let anybody tell you that you can't do something, you can't go to this class or you can't be a part of this or you can't learn. And there was a lot of times with things like—we always just assume that we're not able to learn something or that we don't know something. People always assume that you're stupid, not as educated as somebody else was, they don't really know your background. . . . And really when people underestimate you, I find when people underestimate you, that's when you use that, but be able to back up what you know. So I would just say go to school, get educated. I would tell my kids to go to college, go get your MBA, go get your PhD, keep going.

The other notable characteristic expected of the student in the educational transaction is a focus on the purpose of the transaction. The participants shared that students are expected to keep their "eyes on the prize" and work to get good grades and "get that piece of paper" regardless of anything else that is taking place in their life.

Georgette is the mother of a young son and has also taken custody of her eight-year-old nephew, Darius. The boy has experienced an unstable home life with his mother and now has to adjust to a new home, lifestyle, and behavioral expectations. In addition, Darius struggles significantly with reading. As Georgette and I conversed, Darius sat at the table in the adjacent room working on his homework. In a hushed tone, Georgette talked about meeting privately with Darius' teacher. She talked with the teacher about Darius' situation and made arrangements to share as much information as she could make available. Georgette also made it a point to call the teacher to let her know when Darius was off to a rough start for the day.

Although Georgette worked behind the scenes to assist Darius, she made it a point to instill in him his responsibility to learn and embrace education as the key to his future well-being.

> The message that we gave Darius when he got here was that—he's gotten several messages along the way, but we basically told him that there were gonna be things that he was gonna have choices on, and things he was not gonna have choices on. And I was like, "And two of the things that you will not have a choice on is school and church. Absolutely no choice. You have to go, and you have to be respectable, and you have to do your work."
>
> We also tell him that you have to try. Us seeing a blank answer on your math test is not trying. That's just telling me that you looked at it and thought it was too hard and didn't wanna do it. If you try and you get an F, I won't be upset with you because then we can figure out what you need to learn. But if you don't try and you get an F, you're in trouble because you didn't try, not because you got the F.
>
> So that's one thing that [my husband] made sure that he told him. When he comes with his math book and needs help and I don't like math, and we've just been having a time because I had to think of an example, and I was like we gotta correct the ones you did wrong and do the ones you didn't do. And I was mad. I was so mad. But we got it done, so now he's in heaven. I was like, "You gotta bring that book home every night. I don't care if you do it in class, I still wanna see it, so bring it home."

Tales of Redemption

Students in the purposeful educational transaction do not always engage in the transaction or maintain their focus on the purpose of education. Indeed, in many cases, the participants shared instances in which they suffered from lapses in effort, behavior, and personal responsibility. All participants were asked to talk about a time when they got in trouble at school and how their families reacted. However, in a few cases, the participants discussed their challenges and mistakes spontaneously. I found this to be compelling because the participants shared these stories when simply asked to "talk to me about your experiences as a student." The redemption tales shared by Janiece, Paulette, Kevin, and Trig provide some additional insight into the discourse on the role of students.

Janiece went through what she described as a "rebellious period" during her middle school years. When her academics began to suffer, Janiece tried to protect herself from the consequences she knew would come from her family by changing her grades.

Seventh grade was my rebel burst. In seventh grade I actually thought of repeating. I think it was just getting mixed in with the wrong crowd. Half the time I knew the information, just didn't want to do the homework. I'd just rather talk and do nothing, which obviously was gonna cause the bad grades and cause me to fail, and I didn't like it because I was embarrassed.

So I straightened up. It was viewed very negatively, and I guess at that time my great-grandmother was living. So my uncle when I would bring home my report card, I would change the grade. My great-grandmother didn't—if she caught onto it, she didn't say nothing. But when my uncle would say, "Where's your report card?" I never wanted to pull it out. So when he would see it, he would say, "Well, why does it look like this?" I would say, "I don't know. That's how they wrote it"—and my great-grandmother was like, "Oh, it's okay."

It was proven that I had been changing it. I don't know how else to describe it. That's about it. Great-grandmother and I think again, it's just the time she came up in. It was kind of like, 'Oh, that's okay. She didn't do.' But my uncle was on it. He was on it. That was, yes. . . . I would say from my great-grandmother and my mother, it was more disappointment. And my uncle, he was a little harder on me because obviously, it did mean I was being dishonest. So he was hard. So I wouldn't say I got into trouble, but it was just something, something about my uncle and the talking. That was trouble to me, so I just kind of got talked to.

Janiece slipped into this rebellious period even though her family taught her the importance of education. She was pushed to achieve more than her parents who had not attended college. The expectation of her parents was for her to "go to college and make something of myself. Don't get comfortable with mediocre, always try for more." She also had an uncle who continually held her accountable and pushed her to be her best. Her family continued to support her and hold her accountable even though her attitude had changed.

In addition to her family, Janiece was fortunate to have teachers who cared enough and knew her well enough to intervene. Not only did they provide discipline, but they also provided personal supports.

I can remember when I was kind of struggling if I wanted to continue. I was interested in school, but just, like I said, took on this attitude like I wasn't. And I remember there was this one teacher. It was actually several teachers, and I don't know if it's because they knew my parents or what the case was at one time. I remember them pulling me to the side and basically telling me, I needed to straighten up.

It was one-on-one. I needed to straighten up, and they know the way I was acting as just being rebellious because at that time, I was actually raised by my great-grandparents. And my grandmother she had gotten really sick. So I guess out of anger, some of the things I was doing was just because. So they just said; it was like, "I know you're interested in college. This isn't gonna get you there if you don't straighten up." So then, I wound up getting in a program called the One-up Mentoring Program, and I started off with a mentor, and she really helped me. She was very positive, and I actually wound up being a mentor. So that's kind of how it went.

This kind of intervention to support students is one of the things expected of teachers in the educational transaction.

Whereas some of the participants had one major instance of a lapse in judgment, behavior, or responsibility, several others simply recognized that they did not take advantage of all of the opportunities that were available to them during their teenage years. Many times this was due to a lack of understanding of how their choices would affect them in the future. Ralph, Mena, and Daniel each confessed that they would take advantage of all of the opportunities and support that was available to them in middle and high school if they were able to do it all over again. Paulette talked about her a decline in her grades during her high school years.

I got straight A's in grammar school, until I got to high school. And then . . . my mom passed when I was in eighth grade. . . . After she passed away, my grades slipped. And in high school, I was a straight C student because I lost confidence. I didn't think I could do really well. The opportunity was given to me. I didn't excel. I didn't take advantage of that opportunity to learn more and to take advantage of all the different types of classes that were offered, and things like that, so that I can expand my knowledge.

Kevin attended a magnet school that he described as one of "the top five schools in the community." He was the only African American boy in his classes, he experienced the pressure of being in classes that were not attended by any of his friends. Although he cared about performing well academically, Kevin did not fully engage in the educational process.

Looking back at it I wish I had have took advantage of some of the opportunities that I didn't take advantage of while going to those magnet schools because they offered a lot as far as learning. You know, I personally believe that you pick up some of your habits that you develop early on early in life. Early, you know, in your childhood years. You know, when you're in your elementary school, you know, trying to get there, you know.

And once again, being the only African American at this magnet school of White students, but they're the only ones in this classroom and so forth and the [African American] teachers are not there, as you well know, you don't have that person, that influence to push you. You know, should you? I guess you really shouldn't, but it seems like the other kids may have gotten more of the help. Well, you know you've got to get help. You don't need a babysitter but sometimes you need that encouragement, you need that example, you know.

People need an example. They need to see something in order to know that they can achieve. What I mean by seeing is being able to talk to somebody they can respect that has been through what they've been through or similar situations.

Now that the participants are responsible adults, they are able to reflect on their lapses. Although they experienced some difficulty for a short time, they overcame their lapses and successfully completed their educations.

One of the participants shared how his pattern of poor judgment and troublesome behavior continued from elementary school through young adulthood. I met Trig at a coffee shop during the busiest time of the day. He is a soft-spoken, articulate man of 34. Trig always showed academic potential, but he got sidetracked by the realities of his dual life. Trig went through upper elementary, middle school, high school, and college as a student and a gang member. His lapses into criminal behavior almost ruined his opportunity for an education.

Trig is an exemplar of a recurring theme of redemption shared by the participants.

> I grew up on 55th Street in Chicago. At a very young age, it was a nice community, by the time I reached fifth grade, I saw gang banging, people selling drugs, lot of fighting, so I kind of grew up thinking that that was an acceptable way of life. Although my parents worked, it was hard for me to understand their point of view of things because everybody else in the community was involved in—like I caught my first case in eighth grade. [I had] several other run-ins with the law when I was in high school. Actually had a plastic lens put in my left eye from fights, ended up scratching my own lens, I couldn't see. [I] had gun cases in high school, that type of thing, but was always a good student in spite of it.

Indeed, Trig was a very capable student who experienced two extremes of the educational system. He attended an outstanding parochial school for kindergarten and first grade, went to public school in second grade, and attended a combination of parochial schools and magnet schools. Trig demonstrated high ability and occasional misbehavior at each of the schools.

> I enjoyed school when I was in first grade, I learned a lot. My mom was a teacher so she pretty much taught me everything, but—so there's not really a specific incident, but just that experience I remembered more into second grade, my first two years I was in a Catholic school.
>
> When I went to second grade, I went to the public school in the neighborhood, that's when I realized the difference. In fights every day, I was a smaller kid, so—with a big mouth—so. Lots of fights. One in particular, I got bit by

a young lady, and it was a non-issue for the teacher, for the class, and when I went to Catholic school and we got into a fight, they would call the parents, that same time. This school they just kind of ignored because like—deal with it, you know?

Third grade, I got suspended for pulling a cap gun in class, shooting a couple of—a cap. That was memorable because of the effect that it had. I was back in Catholic school in third grade. And then it was a huge response, whereas kids did stuff like that all the time when I was in second grade in the public school, didn't seem like a big deal.

Just, my mom being an educator, she was serious about education. When I went to public school, we watched a movie a week, there'd be times when— well actually, I don't remember the length of time, but I know that we generally had substitute teachers as much as we had a normal teacher in class, just not a lot of education going on.

In third grade, Trig learned to love reading. His teacher inspired him by having him read Greek mythology and leading discussions about books. During that same year, Trig started "gang banging." He described the strange expectations of the gang leaders.

Most of the older members mandated that we attended school. They promoted a lot of things that weren't good, but that was something that was always communicated, we wouldn't be outside hanging out during the day, we had to go to school. And even at—even to some extent in high school they'd come and get me and drop me off at school, those kinds of things. The hard part wasn't necessarily the members of my gang; it was the competing gangs and other people that we were in conflict with that made it difficult. You always worry about them showing up outside of school when you getting out, and since I went to a magnet high school, there may have been one or two other members in the school.

In most cases, Trig was able to hide the extent of his activities from his parents, but he made note of one time he got caught. As a high school freshman, Trig went to school drunk and his father had to come to school to pick him up. His parents held him accountable and punished him, but Trig was not yet ready to change his behavior.

I kind of grew up in a household where I knew that I was gonna pay for things and so I really would just do everything to subject myself to the discipline. But there were times when I would pick and chose, like I'd know that I was gonna get in trouble for something and I'd make a decision and this particular time was one of those times.

I think that was a big part of my ability to go off and do my homework when I know I needed to and things because my gang banging and things really weren't focused on by my parents because my academic performance usually masked that type of stuff. But it was like, "Trig's doing good in school, he works," so it wouldn't appear that I was doing a lot of things that I was.

Despite his gang membership, Trig remained engaged enough in the educational transaction to complete high school and continue on the college. His parents were convinced that he was doing okay and not one of his teachers knew him well enough to intervene.

Actually, I brought the gang banging with me to college. A lot of people at [the university] being from the city had gang affiliations and that actually continued for a while. I actually ended up being incarcerated while at college. It's not necessarily a gang-related incident, but I got arrested because of robbing and stealing, behaviors that I brought with me from Chicago. That time that I had to think about the opportunity that I had wasted because I performed well in college even while gang banging, 3.2 GPA, but drinking and partying good months in a row. I think that realizing the opportunity that I had wasted is what made me decide that I had to go ahead and finish a degree and get a job.

Trig was fortunate to have the opportunity to redeem his opportunities after he got out of prison. Now a successful college graduate who works with young people through the Big Brothers, Big Sisters program, Trig tries to guide other young people.

[We talk about] the importance of getting an education, the importance of performing well academically, the habits, and—not only the habits, but the character you have to develop to overcome some of the obstacles that you kind of encounter pursuing a degree or watching and learning things. One of the biggest issues that I have with African American students in Big Brother, Big Sister. And a lot of the problem cases that are coming through Big Brother, Big Sister are in troubled homes, it's about deciding what it is you want for yourself rather than being lead by television commercials, by popular cultures that don't evaluate things objectively.

I think about my gang banging and things we did in the past, me and my fellow gang bangers. We didn't control anything in our lives. Communities weren't—we didn't own—there weren't Black men that owned the businesses, the school teachers, the policeman were all the different races. The only control that we had was our ability to inflict fear and pain amongst our own peers. We got so caught up in the idea of being respected, rather than being respectful.

It's the same thing that I see now with kids that want the gym shoes and rims—not that they don't look nice, I enjoy some of those things myself—but just the idea that you can—that you're actually responsible for your wants and desires. That you have to want to do well in school, you have to want to go to— you have to want to get an education. It's not as easy as getting a scholarship so you don't you have to pay to show up to class and get good grades. You actually have to put in work. I think that a lot of it is just that we don't have the willing-ness to put in the effort to earn the things that we say we want just isn't there.

After the lapse, Trig eventually recovered and personalized the expecta-tions that had been held by his parents. This pattern was also shared by other participants. Key to the participants' redemption was the fact that their lapse did not permanently close their doors of opportunity. Their parents and teachers neither stepped in to "save" these young people nor wrote the student off as a lost cause. They continued to provide opportunities for the student to live up to high expectations. The idea that students can be reen-gage in the process of education, refocus on the purpose of education and redeem their role in the purposeful educational transaction is an important aspect of this framework.

CONDUCTING THE TRANSACTION

The role of each participant in the purposeful educational transaction is critical to the success of the transaction, as are the interrelationships between the roles. The educational transaction can only take place with the relation-ships between individuals intact. Although the role of each participant is significant, they are not equal. Instead, the roles are distinct, interdependent, and proportional. The amount of effort or "force" exerted in the three roles is worth exploring. Proportionally, the teacher's role demands the greatest amount of effort or force.

Without the effort provided by the teacher, the lever is ineffectual. Oper-ating within the role of the fulcrum, the parent has no ability/opportunity to exert force to directly lift the student without the efforts of a teacher. A fulcrum is defined as "the support or point of support on which a lever turns in raising or moving something" or "a means of exerting influence, pressure, etc." (Webster, 1986). The parent is responsible for supporting the transaction and applying the necessary influence and pressure to bear the student.

Similarly, the force provided by a teacher will have no direct effect on the student without the fulcrum of expectations provided by the parent. This fact coincides with the common idea that parent involvement is critical to student success. However, for African American community members, par-ent involvement is not focused on assisting with the "work" of education. Instead, it is focused on supporting the transaction by raising expectations for the student and the teacher. The student is part of the purpose of the edu-cational transaction as well as being the primary recipient of the good and service of education.

The educational transaction is also dependent on the student engaging and persevering in the transaction. The effort expected from students is focused inward and upward. To engage in the process the student must value the good and service of education and embrace a sense of purpose.

The relationships that comprise the purposeful educational transaction have the potential to ensure student success. However, the purposeful educational transaction is fragile because the failure of any one part of the system results in the breakdown of the entire transaction. This idea is helpful in understanding how the 15 African American community members analyze the existence of an outcome gap.

Analysis of the Outcome Gap

The participants analyzed the outcome gap as the result of a breakdown in the purposeful educational transaction. The breakdown could be caused by any participant in the transaction refusing, forsaking, or being ineffective in their role. Responsibility and blame for a failed transaction can be assigned to the teacher, the parent, or the student.

Lack of teacher caring and effort renders the educational transaction fruitless. Because the educational transaction is highly dependent on the work of the teacher and the relationship between the teacher, student, and parent, the African American community members view a lack of caring and effort on the part of the teacher to be a major cause of lagging academic achievement for African American youth. This deficit is compounded by a lack of understanding of African American children's lives and culture.

Missy's advice for improving the outcomes for African American youth revolved around the effort and efficacy of teachers.

> All the teachers need to be evaluated on how they are teaching the students. Are you actively engaging the students, or are you just sitting there, just handing out a piece of paper and telling them to do it, no explanation? How are your students achieving? Are all of them getting good grades? Or not just grades because sometimes, grades can be manipulated. Are they learning? How can they apply what they're learning to everyday life?"

Mena placed the same emphasis on teacher efficacy, but she recognized the need for teachers to become culturally competent in order to meet the needs of African American children.

> There's just not a lot of connection that's being made there. . . . It all boils down to having a culturally competent curriculum. It's not just for our kids, but more importantly, for our teachers as well—for them to be culturally competent enough

to be able to know how to teach. We're all human beings. We're all the same people, but the culture of people is something that's unique, and something that we could—if we learn about, it could add to the learning process for both parties.

The standard for teacher efficacy in the purposeful educational transaction is based on the teacher's work with individual children. To be successful in teaching, the teacher must build a relationship with the student, learn how to motivate the student, and do what it takes to empower the student. Mena's hopes for her child's teachers demonstrated the deficit that she saw in the average teachers' work with African American youth.

I think I would like for my child's teacher to know how to help in the process . . . help them to be proud of who they are, and give them a positive message about African Americans and other cultures as a whole—to have the ability to show them how to enjoy the learning process, and to be able to get the messages out of that, and to utilize them in all aspects of their lives. I think that's what I would like for my kid as far as a teacher would be concerned. Someone who could empower, who has the ability to motivate and empower people to bring out something within my child that they already have, with me being a partner in that—us working together to help this child reach his full potential.

It's a very difficult thing to do, but I think that's definitely the way we need to move in, is giving teachers the skills and ability to do that, and not making it so difficult for them to do their jobs. I know it's not easy. I make this sound like it's all on the teachers because it's not. They have a very difficult task. I commend them for what they are able to do, but I think working together with that, so they can start the class right at the beginning. They don't have to spend so much time shutting them up, and getting lessons going. Then making [teachers] culturally competent, so that they understand how to tap into sources of motivation or excitement in kids, and being able to identify and relate to messages back to things that maybe more within one culture versus another.

Something that they can click within a kid because it's something that's tradition within their home—oh yeah, okay, I know what you're talking about because we do that. Being able to have those—that information to pull from so that they can bring that out in a kid and motivate them or relate the message to something that they identify with.

Blame for the failure of the transaction can also be placed on parents. The 15 African American community members also hold high expectations for parents to monitor and support the transaction. Parents are to establish strong expectations for their children and hold their children and the teachers accountable for their performance. The transaction is based on home-based parent involvement, which is defined as setting expectations for behavior and grades, reacting swiftly when the teacher expresses concern about behavior or grades, and making sure the student attends school and completes homework.

Parent involvement also includes monitoring to ensure that the teacher is executing his/her role appropriately.

When parents are not present or they abandon or are ineffective in this role, underachievement is likely to result. The participants recognized the failure of parents to fulfill their role as a major cause of failure of the transaction. Missy, Dudley, Mena, and others expressed disappointment in what they saw as an increase in parents abandoning their proper roles. Mark commented on the failure of parents.

> Some parents just let their kids run all over them. I mean, you see little kids out at all times of night, cussing and fighting and how are those kids gonna do in school? And the parents wonder why the kid is always in trouble. If you can't control them, how do you expect the teacher to do it? My mom would've never let me get away with stuff like that. The teacher better not have to call home. You better act like you got some sense. Now some of the kids don't have to answer to anybody. They end up out there in the streets. Well, if they don't answer to mama, they will end up answering to the police.

Students can also cause the breakdown of the transaction. Because the student's role in the purposeful educational transaction is to focus on the purpose of education, the student is particularly vulnerable to distractions stemming from the community and the society. A student must believe in the purpose of education and embrace the traditional African American cultural value of education as a way to individual, family, and community uplift. This belief is supported by the student's immersion in the discourse of perseverance and struggle. In addition, like the teacher and parent, the student must engage in the transaction in order for it to take place.

The 15 African American community members identified confusion or lack of knowledge about African American history, immersion in a societal normalization of failure for African Americans, and a focus on short-term gain as reasons contributing to the breakdown of the transaction and the pesrpetuation of the achievement gap.

Identity confusion is a condition that causes African American youth to embrace a skewed, negative view of themselves, their community, and their culture. It is exacerbated by the achievement gap ideology. Mena spoke about the need or African American young people to receive a positive message from all sources to combat identity confusion. She noted the importance of the stories that are told to, about, and in the presence African American young people.

> I would definitely change the message and empower them, especially—we don't always hear the good. We don't always hear the positive stories, and I would like for them to hear more about that, and hear more about how strong

are the people that they come from, and how we've endured, and been able to rise above, and succeed, and hear more of those success stories, and see more of that within our communities. It just shows you that it doesn't matter socially or economically where you're coming from. We still need to give that message to our children all across the board, and know that they have that ability, that we're more than bling-bling, and all that stuff that unfortunately our society is made of today.

Unfortunately, African American young people are keenly aware of the statistics regarding the outcome gaps between African Americans and Whites. Being surrounded by stories and statistics of failure can cause pessimism about one's own abilities and chances. This normalization of failure for African American youth causes a negativity that Missy identified.

I tend to see and know a lot of people that are negative, that are African-American. They're very negative, and they're not placed with positive people and influences around them to let them know that they can achieve anything or give them some kind of hope, some kind of dream, to give them something to look forward to.

The participants' personal views also reflected what I found to be a disturbing level of pessimism about the future of the ideal of social and educational equality. Generations of struggling for educational equality have left the 15 African American community members doubting the larger society's professed belief in equality and "color-blindness."

In addition to blaming teachers, parents, and students for the breakdown of the educational transaction, the participants also identified the views of the larger society as the culprit. Stereotypes and the low expectations they produce contribute to the outcome gap and the achievement gap ideology. In addition, stereotypes stemming from the achievement gap ideology destroy the purposeful educational transaction by limiting each participant's effectiveness in playing his/her role in the transaction starting with the student. When asked how society could change to improve educational outcomes for African American students, all of the 15 participants listed eliminating negative stereotypes as a necessary change. They also commented that "it won't happen."

One could argue that the outcome gap is the result of a vicious cycle perpetuated by a refusal to engage in the educational transaction. Faced with a breakdown of the educational transaction and an achievement gap ideology that seems to preclude a successful relationship between African American parents and teachers, African American parents find themselves trying to mediate a transaction without the power or influence to negotiate the transaction. This leaves parents to play the only role they have left within their conceptual framework of education. This means they have to focus their energy on upholding expectations for the student and for the teacher.

Without a relationship of equality, mutual respect, and trust between the parent and the teacher, the parent is very likely to favor the role of protecting the students from perceived injustices perpetrated by teachers and schools instead of supporting the educational transaction by holding positive expectations. As a result, African Americans gain a reputation of being confrontational with teachers and administrators. This makes teachers and school personnel even more reluctant to engage in a transaction with parents. The breakdown of thousands of individual educational transactions, the failure of schools, parents, and students to engage in the transaction due to a lack of trust, and a societal refusal to confront the achievement gap ideology results in the perpetuation of the outcome gap.

I have proposed the purposeful educational transaction as a conceptual framework to aid in the understanding of the participants' discourse about education. This framework is a way to think about the process of education as discussed by the participants. I have described the distinct roles and responsibilities of parents, teachers, and students within the educational transaction framework, and I have discussed the participants' analyses of the outcome gap in light of these roles.

In the final chapter of this work, I will conclude by discussing the ongoing role the achievement gap ideology plays in the education of African American children and how this ideology interacts with the purposeful educational transaction and other counternarratives.

Chapter 5

The Fundamental Conflict

The patterns of belief and action that originated the achievement gap continue to this day. The achievement gap ideology is so ingrained in the life of American society that it has been embraced in schools, universities, communities, and homes even by the most virtuous souls who really would like to see equality in American society. The ideology is self-perpetuating and the outcome gaps only serve to support the ideology among people who do not know any better. Schools, educators, researchers, politicians, and policymakers continue to try to "help" African American children while embracing the achievement gap ideology to the extent that they see no need to ask African Americans "How can I help?"

There is one school of thought that says "respect" is treating others the way you want to be treated. Do unto others as you would have them do unto you. But there is another school of thought that says true respect is treating others the way *they* want to be treated. In schools, the current emphasis on colorblindness results in educators treating all children in a way that reflects the beliefs, values, and desires of the White middle class with little or no recognition that this does not demonstrate respect for all children. This contributes to the outcome gap.

In this chapter, I conclude by discussing the ways in which the purposeful educational transaction framework can influence the way educators, researchers, and local policymakers discuss, research, and address the outcome gap and the achievement gap ideology. In the first section, I review the elements of the purposeful educational transaction that can serve as a new narrative about African American education. In the next section, I propose ways in which the purposeful educational transaction conflicts with the achievement gap ideology and the structures and beliefs that support it. I expose the assumption that failure is a default for African American students and present examples of quality research that counters this narrative. I also share my own perspective on the conflict between the purposeful educational transaction and the "mainstream" view of education. I go on to argue what it means to "help" African American children and advance my views on the role the purposeful educational transaction framework should play in this process. Lastly, in a section that I have titled "Every Goodbye Ain't Gone," I present some final thoughts for those interested in closing the "achievement gap."

THE PURPOSEFUL EDUCATIONAL TRANSACTION AS A NEW NARRATIVE

I have presented the purposeful educational transaction as a new narrative or framework aimed at allowing a truly respectful exploration of the process of educating African American children. This framework places the views of the 15 African American community members I interviewed in the center of the discussion.

Based on the educational transaction framework, I argue that education can be viewed as a transaction in which a good is conferred on the recipient through the service of teaching. I describe this view using economic terminology because this framework links education with empowerment, social capital, and personal and community economics. The educational transaction is described as purposeful because the 15 participants spoke about obtaining an education for the specific purpose of personal and community uplift instead of discussing education as a good unto itself.

Within the framework that I propose, the roles of parents, teachers, and students are distinct and interrelated. Based on the voices of the participants, I have placed parents as the fulcrum of the transaction, where they play the role of setting expectations for the student and the teacher. Numerous comments and stories inspired me to cast the teacher as the source of force or effort. Indeed, the 15 African American community members communicated strong expectations for teachers based on shared views of what it means to teach.

In considering the role of students in the participants' discourse, I have described the student as the recipient of the effort and leverage from the teacher and parent. The participants expected students to embrace the purpose of education, fight to overcome, and focus their efforts on individual and community uplift. I included some of the participants' tales of redemption as a way to further explicate the student's role in engaging and reengaging in the transaction.

Operating within the framework of the purposeful educational transaction as a new narrative about the education of African American children leads to a distinctive analysis of the existence of the outcome gap. I have proposed that the 15 African American community members I interviewed analyzed the outcome gap as a result of a breakdown of the educational transaction caused by the failure of one or more parties to fulfill their role. The roles of parents, teachers, and students are equally crucial to the transaction. If parents do not provide expectations, if teachers do not demonstrate the effort and caring to "teach," or if students do not engage in the transaction, negative outcomes will result. Although the African American community values education, each party to the educational transaction is also bombarded by the achievement gap ideology that persists in American society.

The participants' stories suggest that the educational transaction can recover from students' lapses in judgment, behavior, or engagement when the student achieves redemption. In addition, although the participants' demonstrated some disdain for parents who fail to uphold expectations, it appeared that it was possible for other adults such as other family members and mentors to assume this role. The 15 African American community members' analysis of the outcome gap included the failure of educators to effectively play their roles in the transaction. The participants spoke of the parent's role in setting expectations for the teacher; however, the purposeful educational transaction provides no recourse for African American community members when teachers do not fulfill their role.

By engaging the new narrative of African American education as a purposeful educational transaction, researchers, practitioners, and local educational policymakers can approach closing the outcome gap in ways that reject Whiteness and respect the African American community. The purposeful educational transaction framework allows analysis of the outcome gap that goes beyond the assertion of achievement gap ideology that African American educational success is an exception to the rule.

A FUNDAMENTAL IDEOLOGICAL CONFLICT

The purposeful educational transaction framework that I advance is fundamentally opposed to the achievement gap ideology and the structures that support it. The unique perspective of African Americans has a tremendous effect on the experiences African American community members have in schools. If we are to make use of this information, then we must consider how this framework conflicts with the discourse on education in public schools and in society as a whole.

Throughout this study, I have made the argument that schools have been designed to meet the needs of White middle-class society in all aspects including the way schools are designed, the way teachers interact with students, the expectations for parents, the curricular decisions, and the school's interaction with the community. The African American discourse on education and the achievement gap presents educators and local policymakers with an important challenge. Presented with the beliefs and values of these 15 African American community members, educators must decide whether they will make the African American community central to the process of turning all schools into places where African American children will learn and succeed. The alternative is to continue to subject Black children to the enduring achievement gap ideology.

I have defined the achievement gap ideology as a social construct based on the racist societal belief that the quantifiable differences in educational, social, and economic scores and outcomes of the different races are based on "true"/"real," authentic differences in ability, potential, viability, and proclivity. By tracing the development and perpetuation of this ideology in the historical discourse and traditional research, I have demonstrated that the achievement gap ideology has undergone a metamorphosis during its history. This metamorphosis involved changing from an overt argument based on biological characteristics to a pseudo-altruistic argument based on social development, and now to an implicit assumption that has been accepted as a simple "matter of fact." This latest evolutionary stage in the development of the achievement gap ideology is the most insidious and difficult to confront in a society in which no one wants to be called a racist.

Not only do schools continue to exist in the form that was originally designed to socialize students into Whiteness and to sort them based on desirability, but current school policies are established based on historical assumptions made over time. The current form of the achievement gap ideology is based on five principles:

1. Differences among "races" and "classes" are authentic and affect student learning. Black, Hispanic, and poor students are less able. (To be politically correct, when educators discuss this idea, race is replaced with the words "low income," "at-risk" or "urban.")
2. Individual potential can be measured and predicted. (Potential is defined by those in the "mainstream.")
3. The end goal of schools is to sort students and educate them based on their measured/predicted potential.
4. Certain values are "right" and should therefore be universal. Disagreement with these "universal" values is a sign of immorality, impaired judgment, or inferiority.

5. Failure is a default for some children, particularly those who do not embrace "universal" values and those who lack "potential."

Educators, administrators, educational policymakers, and parents have been immersed in this achievement gap ideology in their own schooling and in their training. Many have also experienced previous iterations of the ideology.

Failure as a Default

Principles one through four in the current achievement gap ideology are used to justify principle five—failure as a default. This is the idea that perpetuates the gap. The achievement gap ideology makes the failure of African American and low-income students expected and commonplace. Hence, there is no urgency to close the achievement gap, nor is there any societal or institutional memory of success for these groups. When African American children enter a new school or classroom, years of social, political, and economic history tell educators (well meaning though they may be) that Black children's potential is limited and that they will be the exception if they succeed. As long as this is the case, Black children will continue to be held prisoner by the default of failure.

When a group of children are expected to fail, it is easy to make decisions that hurt their chances. It is easy to establish "zero tolerance" policies that make messing up ruinous. It is not a big deal to observe the prevalence of their failure. In fact, their failure does not tell us anything about the schools they attend. It simply provides more evidence for their limited potential. When failure is the default, planning to help the students succeed is a waste of valuable time and effort that could otherwise be spent on those with a chance of succeeding. When failure is the default, the demand to "close the achievement gap" is absurd because those kids will probably fail anyway.

When failure is the default, it is okay to provide children with a substandard education that does not prepare them for higher education because most of them are not "college material." Then it is perfectly appropriate to use "affirmative action" policies to enroll a limited number of them in college when it fulfills our purpose. If they subsequently fail, we can say, "See, I told you so." If they succeed, we can say they are only there because they are Black.

The folly of the No Child Left Behind Act is not the specifics of the law. It is not the specter of accountability. It is not even the goal of 100 percent proficiency (although this idea flies in the face of the achievement gap ideology). The true folly of the No Child Left Behind Act is the fact that beliefs cannot be legislated. People who believe African American children are doomed to failure will make decisions for their own self-interest and in the interest of children who seem to be destined for success and not in the interest of the African American child. Educators' faulty belief systems are what convince them that the only way to get Black children to make "AYP" is to drill them with low-level skills. It is also what inspires them to be offended by the idea that they are accountable for outcomes for all students.

The default of failure causes children to see themselves in the way they have been portrayed. It means the chorus of expectations they may receive from parents is drowned out by frequent examples of "failure as predicted." It means that to succeed young people have to strive to be the exception or outlier at precisely the time of life that fitting in is most important. It means being immersed in an environment in which they are the very image of "at-risk," and "gifted" looks nothing like them at precisely the time they are exploring what it means to be who they are.

Failure as a default means parents can be filled with as much fear as hope when looking at their young children because they know that their brown skin and curly hair will cost them. It makes parents mistrust and want to fight the system that relegates their children to special education, detention, or school suspension. As long as failure is seen as the default for African American children, the achievement gap ideology will reign in American society and the outcome gap will remain.

Countering the Narrative

People seldom question values and ideas that are thought to be universally accepted. It is essential that the societal embrace of the achievement gap ideology be confronted by thoughtful researchers and practitioners who understand the role that ideology plays in research and practice. William Watkins (2001) wrote of the power of ideology:

> Ideology is not left to chance. . . . Hence, ideology becomes the currency of those dominating the culture. Ideology is imparted subtly and made to appear as though its partisan views are part of the "natural order." The dominating ideology is a product of dominant power. (p. 9)

There has been a growing chorus of researchers who have questioned the dominant ideology and offered alternative ways of conducting research with African American community members, framing African American education, and addressing what is known as the "achievement gap." As Michael Apple (1990) asserted, "We have nearly totally depoliticized the culture that schools distribute. Yet there is a growing body of curriculum scholars and sociologists of education who are taking much more seriously the questions of "Whose culture?" "What social group's knowledge?" and "In whose interest is certain knowledge (facts, skills, and propensities and dispositions) taught in cultural institutions like schools?" (p. 16). The counternarratives shared by researchers provide ways to confront the achievement gap ideology in popular discourse, educational policy, and educational research.

James Anderson (1989) presents a counternarrative to the misguided view in popular discourse that African American culture devalues education. In his work titled *The Education of Blacks in the South, 1860–1935*, Anderson gives an account of the many inequities that plagued Black education after slavery including funding disparities, poor facilities, shorter school years, and inadequate books and resources. However, the throughline of his work is the commitment that African Americans showed to fighting for access to education, achieving education as individuals, and improving education in their states.

The efforts of African American community members provided the impetus for improvements in schools, longer school years, better teacher training, and increased resources for education (Anderson, 1989). This commitment to education continues despite the persistence of the achievement gap ideology. By presenting this counternarrative, Anderson promotes a level of understanding of and respect for African American culture that is necessary to enable a productive dialogue about African American education.

In her presidential address to the American Educational Research Association, Gloria Ladson-Billings (2006) advanced the idea of reframing the "achievement gap" as the "education debt." She argued that the same economic principles used to distinguish the national deficit from the national debt could be applied to the idea of the achievement gap. In her view, the main reason for the intractability of the "achievement gap" is the fact that the short-term investments and solutions focused on raising student achievement address the education deficit but leave the long-term education debt untouched. As the education debt is left to fester, it grows with each passing year, resulting in the necessity of investing more and more to simply pay the interest (e.g., crime, violence, etc.) on the education debt.

Ladson-Billings critique of the current discourse on the "achievement gap" serves to shift attention to the societal causes of the outcome gap by focusing the argument on historical and contemporary actions and events instead of on the perceived deficits of the African American community and culture. Ladson-Billings (2006) goes on to advocate addressing the education debt because this is necessary to improve education overall and because failing to do so could result in future educational bankruptcy. By using economic terms such as deficit, debt, and bankruptcy, she encourages researchers and policymakers to consider the connection that education has to economics and to consider the results of the growing education debt in the same ways that they consider the results of the national debt. Ladson-Billings' idea of the education debt offers an analysis of the achievement gap discourse at the national level and provides an impetus for policymakers to begin to think of this issue on different terms.

Many scholars have confronted the achievement gap ideology in educational research and advanced Afrocentric, culturally sensitive, and endarkened perspectives on conducting meaningful research with African American communities (Asante, 1990; Dillard, 2006, King, 2005). In response to the challenges offered by these and other new epistemologies, Scheurich and Young (1997) seek to answer the question "Are our research epistemologies racially biased?" They argue that there is a level of epistemological racism that arises out of the fact that American civilization was grounded in the achievement gap. "A result of this is that these negative distortions pass into the dominant culture as "truth," thus becoming the basis of individual, group, and institutional attitudes, decisions, practices, and policies" (Scheurich & Young, 1997, p. 9). Scheurich and Young suggest that the way to combat epistemological racism is to open a dialogue among scholars on the variety of epistemologies that are available and the ways in which favoring traditional ways of doing research affect the prominence of racial bias in the academy and in American society.

Dillard (2006) advances endarkened epistemology as a way in which African American women approach research and leadership in the academy. She argues that the metaphor of research must change from "research as recipe" taking out the researchers voice and presenting the results as objective truth (Dillard, 2006, p. 663). The endarkened metaphor of research is "research as responsibility" (Dillard, 2006, p. 663). Like Asante, Tillman, and King, she argues that researchers must be held accountable to the community and that they have a responsibility to research with purpose.

Endarkened epistemology embraces and makes use of historical context, personal and cultural identity, emotion, and personal experiences to make sense of the world (Dillard, 2006). When researchers delete their own voices from their research, they assist in supporting the epistemological racism that lingers in the academy. The recognition that the researchers voice and experiences are necessary for meaningful endarkened research has the potential to open up more avenues for dialogue and understanding. Dillard (2006) shares her understanding of the importance of experience.

> In African American communities, what happens in everyday life to individuals within the community is critical to "making sense" of particular actions,

expressions and community life in general. . . . We "study" the concrete experiences and acts of African-Americans or people of color, while at the same time striving to understand and explicate the wisdom contained in those meanings. Thus, concrete experiences—uniquely individual while at the same time both collective and connected—lend credibility to the work of African-American women engaged in transformative research and inquiry. (p. 676)

My Perspective

Following in the footsteps of Asante, Tillman, King, Dillard, and other African/African American researchers, I have presented the purposeful educational transaction as a way of understanding African American education without the lens of Whiteness. Throughout the study, I have made use of African American intellectual tradition, participant voices, personal experience, and my own voice to develop and share a new narrative that is contrary to the achievement gap ideology. The purposeful educational transaction framework brings the analysis of the outcome gap at a level does not solely focus on how we research the gap but also on how African American community members experience, discuss, and make meaning of education and the outcome gap.

The narrative of the purposeful educational transaction was not formulated as a philosophical or theoretical counternarrative. Instead, it is designed to build an understanding of the complex beliefs, values, expectations, and stories shared by the 15 African American community members. The goal of this framework is not to initiate an argument about the merits of African American cultural values in comparison to those of Whites as so often happens. The goal is to challenge educators and local policymakers to think about the education of African American children with the perspectives of African American community members in the center.

The purposeful educational transaction provides a framework of the way the 15 African American community members view education. The process of thinking critically about the system of beliefs that undergirds a group's interaction with the school system is important in exposing the ways in which structures and beliefs support the achievement gap ideology. Based on my own experiences as a student, teacher candidate, teacher, school administrator, district administrator, and parents in predominantly White, middle-class school systems, universities, and communities, I have my own endarkened perspective on the framework of education that is promulgated as "mainstream." I will share this perspective as a way to challenge the reader to think critically about how the "mainstream" framework of education is enacted in schools.

THE FUNDAMENTAL EDUCATIONAL CONFLICT

There is a fundamental conflict that arises when people who view education as a transaction enter a mainstream school system that espouses a different view of the nature of the education process. When views of the purpose and nature of education and the roles and responsibilities of teachers, parents, and students conflict, the relationship is broken and parties refuse to negotiate the educational transaction. Just as our discussion of the purposeful educational transaction took the form of a conceptual framework, the mainstream view of education is a different conceptual framework. Although the "mainstream" view of education is often presented as the standard way of valuing education, this view actually reflects a specific ideology that is promoted within public schools, teacher education programs, professional organizations, and in the media.

My hope is to provide the reader with the opportunity to examine how these conceptual frameworks affect choices made in and about schools. My description of the fundamental conflict is based on my experiences as a student in a predominantly White, middle-class school system, as a teacher candidate in two colleges of education, as a teacher, school administrator, and district administrator. It is also based on elements of the societal conversation about education.

While the 15 African American community members have a clear conception of education as a purposeful transaction, I believe the mainstream view that is supported by schools is that education is an endowment provided to the student from the parent. The use of the term "endowment" is germane because similar to the African American view, the mainstream view of education has a connection to economics. However, the primary actors in this system are the parents.

Parents invest effort, time, energy, money, and influence to endow their children with the best possible education in order to ensure that they maintain a set of qualities and privileges. In this instance, the term "invest" means "to contribute time, energy, or effort to an activity, project, or undertaking in the expectation of a benefit" or "to use money to buy or participate in a business enterprise that offers the possibility of profit, especially by buying stocks or bonds" (Encarta, 2007). To "endow" is to "provide with some talent, quality, etc." and to "give money or property so as to provide an income for the support of" (Webster, 1986).

This view of education coincides with a set of broad values and beliefs known by some as the American Creed. The values are espoused as hallmarks of American culture. The Creed includes the values of equality and civil rights, but these values are mediated by other closely held and vigorously defended values (Watkins, 2001). These values include personal responsibility, competition, and meritocracy. Perhaps, most importantly, the Creed includes intense adherence to ideals of materialism and property rights. Schools were designed to support the values of the creed. In the educational endowment, education is a type of property that parents, through hard work, personal responsibility, and monetary investment, can secure for their children.

This conceptual framework results in different views of the roles of parents, teachers, and students and the interrelationships between those roles. In the educational endowment, parents are directly responsible for the student outcomes and student success. Unlike the educational transaction in which parents are the fulcrum or support, in the educational endowment, the parent exerts the force necessary to make the system work.

Based on my experiences, I view the "mainstream" conceptual framework of education as a pulley system (see Figure 5.1). The parent is the source of force or energy. The teacher acts as the pulley, making the work of the parent easier and more effective. Parents expect teachers to support them by providing their expertise and guidance and by helping parents secure a return on their investment. The school system is critically important because a good school system ensures a higher rate of return on the investment. The

The Educational Endowment

Education is an endowment provided to the student from the parent.

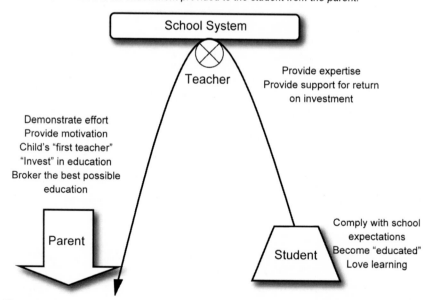

Figure 5.1

student in the educational endowment is responsible to demonstrate compliance, to love learning, and to become educated. "Educated" is the term used for a person who has received the endowment of education and embraced the qualities, attributes, and privileges that go along with the endowment.

In the educational endowment conceptual framework, the parent plays the most important role. The parent embraces the responsibility of being the child's "first teacher." As such, they motivate the student and invest in the school in order to broker the best possible education for the student. Parents see ensuring student academic success as their responsibility. Schools propagate this view of the parent's role by promoting a style of parent involvement that entails spending time at the school, working with their children on specific academic skills, assisting teachers in the classroom as volunteers, and paying for tutors and assistance if necessary.

In our discussion, Ralph noted one difference:

> They assume that everybody's on an equal playing field. That's not the case. Most African American students I know, families I know don't take their kids to Sylvan Learning Center or they don't take their kids to places like other learning centers and other programs like that, because they can't afford it. I've only known two people in my entire life that have been taught by Sylvan Learning Center. . . .
>
> I've also met a lot of students who are trying, but they need extra help in learning. Really, they just need encouragement in helping them to know that they can do the work. If you have a learning disability, that's fine. There are plenty of people that run major corporations and work in the federal government and have become president that have dyslexia and everything else and had other learning disabilities. The only difference is that those families had the resources to actually support and build—make sure that that disability didn't hinder their child's progress. Lower income families and other families with disabilities don't have those resources available. Those resources need to be available to everybody.

The teacher's role in the endowment system is that of support. Teachers provide expertise and specific focus to the education of students. They provide parents with guidelines for working with their children. They also assist in communicating the expectations and values of the parents and the larger society. This is reflected in the vision and mission statements of many school districts that include phrases such as "the school will work in partnership with parents and the community to help students become lifelong learners." In the educational endowment, teachers often play the role or coach or facilitator with the student and the parent. The ideal of constructivism coincides with this conceptual framework.

Expectations for the student's role mirror those of the school system. The student's main responsibility is to receive and show appreciation for the endowment. They are to be compliant, embrace and reflect the values taught at home and at school, take on the characteristics of "educated" people, and become "lifelong" learners. Fighting, struggling, and standing up to opposition are seen as signs of behavior issues as opposed to signs of independence.

In the educational endowment, education is designed to change the student's role and status in society and the community. Being "educated" is defined in terms of the new beliefs, attitudes, behaviors, and status acquired by the student. Schools perpetuate the endowment framework by rewarding and encouraging "good" parents (i.e., parents that invest in the schools in desired ways) and "good" students (i.e., students who comply and perform well).

In what I view as the predominant mainstream view of education as an endowment, the effectiveness of the system is not fully dependent upon the work of the teacher or on the relationship between the teacher and student. Even without the leverage and support provided by the teacher and school system, the parent can still ensure student success. An effective teacher and school system simply makes the endowment process go faster and more smoothly. In this system, only the absence of force or effort from the parent causes the system to break down. This fact makes the educational endowment more robust than the educational transaction.

The view of education as an endowment secured by parents' investments has significant ramifications for the relationship between parents and schools and for the policy decisions at the school, district, state, and federal level. First, the educational endowment frames the purpose of education as perpetuating and passing on privilege and social status. Second, the belief in education as an endowment insinuates that inequality is appropriate and inevitable. Finally, and most importantly, the mainstream view of education as an endowment evokes the idea of scarcity in the imagination of Americans.

The purpose of the educational endowment is ensuring the success of the individual and passing on the knowledge, power, privilege, and status to the next generation. Parents are willing to go to great lengths to ensure a return on their investment in education so that their children will be well endowed with education. This includes "shopping" for schools and investing time, energy, influence, and money to secure the best.

My interaction with Joshua's parents was never very close. Joshua's mother was a frequent volunteer at the school. His father was a well-respected professional who was very involved in the school. Over their few years with children at the school, the family had developed a close friendship with two of the veteran teachers in the building.

After my first year as principal of the school, I changed the placement policy to disallow parent requests for specific teachers based on my belief (stemming from the prior year's experiences) that the school personnel were more capable of making class recommendations based on students' academic needs. With only a few options at each grade level, it was impossible to honor all parent requests while also attending to students' needs. As a part of this new way of doing things, teacher assignments were not to be finalized and posted until the end of the summer a few weeks before the start of the school year.

When the two teachers who were close friends with Joshua's parents violated the policy by moving several other students around so that they could place Joshua in one of their classes, I reversed their decision. I shared with the teacher my concern that she would not be able to treat Joshua the same as other students and that his needs and desires would outweigh those of other students because of their special relationship. The very next morning, I received a call from Joshua's parents asking why I had reassigned their son. I explained my concerns about preferential treatment and used the fact that they knew about their classroom placement four months before any other family and that the teacher had asked them who they would request for a teacher as evidence that this was likely.

Joshua's parent's made it clear that they were "good" parents who contributed a great deal to the school. They moved into the school district for our school purposefully and the mother chose not to work so that she could be an involved parent. She was president-elect of the PTA. She volunteered in the teacher's classroom each day. They raised a great deal of money for the fundraiser. The rules did not need to be applied to them because they were supporters of the school and the kind of parents that I should want to have enroll their children in the school. They made that argument to me, the teacher, and the superintendent before they finally gave up on their request. My relationship with Joshua's parents was forever destroyed.

At the time, I did not understand why Joshua's parents felt that they had a right to be treated differently than other families at the school. The concept that "good" parents (i.e., middle- and upper-class parents who volunteered and otherwise contributed to the school) should be given more respect, privileges, information, and choices than other parents was foreign (and somewhat upsetting) to me.

In hindsight, it makes perfect sense. Operating within the conceptual framework of education as an endowment, Joshua's parents were fulfilling their role of brokering the best possible education to advantage their son. They had made a large investment in the school, and they expected a return on their investment. The teachers, while violating a policy based on education as a transaction, were actually fulfilling their role in the endowment by recognizing Joshua's parents as "good" parents and doing everything they could to support a return on the parents' investment. By stepping in to disallow actions that would promote inequality, I interfered with the process of providing an endowment for their son. No wonder they hated me!

One of the implications of viewing education as an endowment is that inequality is not only acceptable, but also inherent in the system. The parent's job is to ensure that their child is endowed as well as or better than others. In this view, there is no value in trying to ensure that everyone receives an equal education. American society is a meritocracy in which people and their children are rewarded for their success. Parents have a right to make the monetary and other investments necessary to provide their children with the best.

Illinois' system of funding schools through property taxes is supported by this idea. Funding systems that equalize school funding are politically unfeasible because they limit the ability of children to benefit directly from the financial investment of their parents. In the mainstream view, parents have a right to use the public school system to ensure the endowment of their children. Parents who invest their child's community and schools deserve a higher return on their investment. The educational endowment conceptual framework is based on the idea that inequality is the result of the differential investment of parents, whereas, those who subscribe to education as a transaction view inequality as the result of lack of engagement in the educational transaction. This takes the form of low expectations, differential responses to parents, lack of funding, or inadequate teaching.

Perhaps the most important implication of education as an endowment is that the principle of scarcity is applied to the provision of education. Scarcity is an idea from economics that means limited resources are available to meet unlimited wants and needs. In other words, the supply of something that is valued is outweighed by the demand. As a result, the cost rises. When the principle of scarcity is applied to education, it suggests that schools cannot meet the needs of all children. The only way to provide the best possible education for one group is to take something away from another group. An example of this idea is the current backlash against the No Child Left Behind Act led by middle-class parents who feel the emphasis on students who struggle has taken resources from "average" and "gifted" children. In their view, the focus on skills takes away from the focus on creativity and critical thinking.

The application of scarcity to education is detrimental to African American youth because the interests of African Americans tend to lose out when placed in opposition to those of the "mainstream." In the educational transaction framework, scarcity does not apply because the transaction is based on the relationships between individuals. If the individual transaction is supported and successful, it is not affected by the provision of services and programs for others.

The view of education as an endowment that I have described is just one way to critique the "mainstream" framework of education. Other researchers and practitioners may argue that this framework does not adequately represent the values and beliefs inherent in the school system. Certainly, it is based on personal experience and reflection and not past research or data. That said,

Table 5.1.   Elements of Conflict

	Purposeful Educational Transaction	*Educational Endowment*
Teacher Efficacy	Teacher works to ensure the individual student's academic success.	Teacher provides the expertise and support for return on parent's investment.
Parent Involvement	Parent involvement is home-based and includes monitoring the teacher to ensure the best education.	Parent involvement is school-based and includes investing in the school to broker the best education.
Student Success	A student is successful when he perseveres, struggles/fights to overcome, and focuses on social, economic uplift, and empowerment.	A student is successful when he complies with school rules, policies and, values and strives to become "educated."
"Teach"	"Teach" is a verb that means using personal authority to actively direct, lead, and instruct through 'show and tell.'	"Teach" is a verb that means coach, support, and guide through facilitated inquiry and discovery.
"Learn"	"Learn" is a verb that means to acquire specific knowledge, information, and skills and be able to demonstrate them on demand without changing one's role or identity in the community.	"Learn" is a verb that means to engage in a process of discovery, demonstrate creativity, and adopt values, attitudes, and behaviors that reflect those taught.
Scarcity	Benefits to others have no effect on a student's quality of education as long as the individual transaction is adequately supported and successful.	Programs and services provided to others result in an opportunity cost and can result in a decreased return on the parent's investment.

Table 5.1. Elements of Conflict *(continued)*

	Purposeful Educational Transaction	*Educational Endowment*
Equality	Inequality is caused by lack of support for the educational transaction taking the form of poor funding, low expectations, differential responses to parents, or inadequate teaching.	Inequality is caused by differential investment by parents; therefore, it is inherent in the system.
Robustness	The failure of any participant to effectively play the expected role can result in the failure of the entire system.	Only the failure of the parent results in the total failure of the endowment.

this framework reflects how I make meaning of my experiences in predominantly White communities, schools, and institutions of higher learning.

Although some may disagree with the framework that I present, the important thing is that we do indeed critique the accepted "mainstream" view and consider how it affects those with different perspectives. The act of engaging in this kind of critique places the values of the "mainstream" on the same level as those of African Americans and other groups. This is necessary if we are to initiate a dialogue on meeting the needs of African American children.

"HELP"ING AFRICAN AMERICANS

Throughout this study, I have placed African American culture at the center of the discussion. In order to eliminate the outcome gap and combat the achievement gap ideology, researchers, educators, and local policymakers must follow this example. Those who truly desire to eliminate what has been termed as the "achievement gap" must reset the default to success for African American children. Educators must study success, immerse all students in a culture of success, and expose African American children to images of success that look like them.

Educators must also recognize that success is as possible (and probable) for African American children as it is for other children. Administrators and policymakers should stop defining and describing schools based on demographic labels, and they must resist the temptation to expect less of schools that serve African American and low-income students. Moreover, administrators and policymakers have the responsibility to confront those who refuse to take responsibility for the educational outcomes of all students and those

Table 5.2. Do's and Don'ts for Researchers

	Do	*Don't*
Educational Researchers and Policymakers	• Research success among African American students in a variety of settings. Put as much emphasis on determining conditions that promote success as has been put on identifying causes for failure. • Make conversations with African American students, parents, and/or community members an integral part of any research on African American education and the achievement gap. • Study the impact of educational policies on African American students in schools with varying levels of diversity. • Maintain an emphasis on teacher and leader quality. Define quality based on student outcomes and growth.	• Define success for African American children as "better than expected" performance (i.e., better than the "predicted" achievement for African American students). It is inappropriate to replicate programs that provide "better than expected" performance when their performance is still substandard.

who reserve their best efforts for the "good" parents and students. Those who would eliminate the achievement gap must address both the outcome gap and the achievement gap ideology that supports it.

The discourse shared by the participants provides insight into the unique African American community perspective on the roles and responsibilities of each player in the educational system. It also provides us with information about ways in which the achievement gap—so long explored—is analyzed by those who are affected. The unique perspective of African Americans has a tremendous effect on the experiences African American community members have in schools. If we are to make use of this information, then we must consider the implications of the discourse on education in public schools.

Throughout this book, I have made the argument that schools have been designed to meet the needs of White middle-class society in all aspects including the way schools are designed, the way teachers interact with students, the expectations for parents, the curricular decisions, and the school's interaction with the community. The African American discourse on education and the achievement gap presents educators and policymakers with an important challenge. Presented with the beliefs and values of African Americans community members, educators must make a decision on whether they will turn schools into places where African American children will learn and succeed.

In order to close the achievement gap and improve educational outcomes for African American children, we must consider the ways in which we can redesign schools so that they meet the needs and speak to the values of African American community members. The educational discourse shared in this book has implications for schools' expectations for parent involvement, definitions of the teachers' roles and responsibilities, statements of the purpose of education, and reactions to academic and disciplinary problems.

It is important to recognize that the roles of parents, students, and teachers are very distinct in the eyes of members of the African American community. The roles are complementary but separate. The African American community members who participated in the study see themselves as parents, and they distinguish that from teachers. They do not refer to themselves as their child's "first teacher" even though they embrace their importance in their child's education. It is the teacher's job to teach.

In the African American community the most important role of parents in working with young people is setting high expectations and holding both students and teachers accountable for outcomes. It is the parent's expectation that it is the student's job to get an education. It is the student who enters into a transactional relationship with the teacher and the school, and it is their job to follow through on getting the education that is being provided to them.

The participants' discourse suggests that parents feel that it is their job to provide children with a time and place to do homework and to hold them accountable to complete the work. The discourse does not suggest that parents believe they should be teaching children how to do the homework. If the child does not know how to do the homework, it is seen as a problem because the student has not learned what he/she needed to learn in school. In many cases, schools today send home work that requires intensive amounts of hands-on instruction and assistance by parents. Educators must consider that by doing this, they are working in a way that goes against the values and beliefs of African American parents. Parents are willing to assist with homework and help the student practice specific skills; however, instructing the student is seen as interfering with the distinct role of the teacher.

The African American parents in the study did not feel as though they should have to "teach" their children academic skills. These skills should be taught at school. African American parents would then see it as their responsibility to hold out high expectations, to hold children accountable for doing their homework, and to provide children with the supplies they need.

Educators should evaluate the extent to which parents are expected to teach new skills as opposed to enforcing behavioral and academic expectations.

Students should be directly taught a skill and have an opportunity to practice it with support from the teacher prior to taking it home for homework. African American community members tend to believe that teachers should be the experts on teaching. Teachers are seen as having a high level of authority. Therefore, the expectations held for them are high. The tendency of African American parents is to trust educators to make sure that children learn. The basic belief is that teachers should play the role of educating children while parents should pay the role of setting expectations and holding students accountable.

If educators must ask parents to teach academic skills, educators should directly address why they are asking parents to do what parents may consider to be the teachers' job. Otherwise, the teacher will be seen as shirking their responsibilities. Educators should provide parents and students with direct instruction in what educators would like them to do and why. It is important that educators do not make value statements about the roles parents should play.

In addition, the African American community makes a clear distinction between the role of the teacher and that of the parents. When parents are expected to take on the role of a teacher, there is a level of resentment that often arises. This is mirrored in the attitudes of students, who seem to express resentment when they feel as though teachers are abdicating their responsibility to "teach" by choosing to serve as a "facilitator" of learning instead of a teacher.

The relationship between teacher and student is critical, and a great deal of trust is placed in the teacher. When the teacher is seen as betraying that trust by failing to actually teach, it is the parent's responsibility to hold the teacher accountable. Educators must ensure that a strong relationship exists between parent and teacher and teacher and student. African American parents need to implicitly trust the teacher to care for the student, to work hard to ensure that the student learns, to communicate if the student is struggling in some way, and to structure the class and daily instruction in a way that will meet the needs of that individual student. Given that trust, African American parents often think highly of teachers and commend them for doing a difficult job. In the absence of that trust, the relationship breaks down. Because of the extraordinarily strong value African American community members place on the relationship as the basis of learning, if the trust breaks down, learning breaks down as well.

A lack of the traditional parent involvement (i.e., PTO meetings, volunteering in the classroom, etc.) does not indicate a lack of caring about school or a lack of communication with the student about the value of education.

Education is seen as a transaction that takes place between the student and the teacher with the parent as the monitor of the transaction. The African

Table 5.3. Do's and Don'ts for Leaders

	Do	Don't
District and School Leaders	• Disaggregate school and district assessment, discipline, and outcome data. Ask, "Is our school/district providing a quality education?" for each group of students. • Hold all schools and teachers accountable for the outcomes of all students. • Confront low expectations and statements that insinuate that African American and/or low-income students are unlikely to succeed. • Create school- and district-wide homework policies that specifically identify the purpose, scope, time allotments, and expected parent involvement in homework. Share this policy and the reasoning behind it with African American parents and community members. • Train teachers to differentiate instruction (but not expectations) to meet the learning styles and needs of students. Teach teachers multiple instructional methods including direct instruction. Expect teachers to use the methods that work for all of the students they teach and modify them as necessary to get improved outcomes. • Closely examine the equity of access provided across schools. Fund schools in a way that ensures that African American students have equal access to services and resources that promote achievement. (Equal access may require targeted funding.) • Hire high-quality staff members that reflect and support the cultural diversity of the schools. • Get out of your comfort zone of expecting parents to support the school on the school's terms. Go out and meet them where they live (literally and figuratively).	• Use racial diversity or economic disadvantage as an excuse for poor outcomes or low test scores. • Establish "zero tolerance" policies that make suspension and expulsion the expected form of discipline regardless of the circumstances behind the behavior. • Hide low achievement and poor outcomes for African American children behind strong "overall" test scores. "Good" schools must be good for ALL students. • Make decisions about resources and services based on students who "count" for accountability. Every child counts. • Allow staff members to disrespect students by belittling them or using threats, sarcasm, or intimidation. Educators treat students based on their expectations for the students' futures and their respect for students' parents. • Assign ineffective or marginal teachers to African American or low-income students.

American community members in the study place little emphasis on other personnel in the school if the relationship is intact and the transaction is working. The school administration is only meaningful to the extent that it creates and environment that supports the transaction between the teacher and the individual student. This places a great amount of responsibility on the teacher, who is responsible to make sure the student learns. If the student engages in the transaction but does not learn, blame is laid on the teacher. This is particularly the case if the parent has fulfilled his/her responsibility to set high expectations and if the child is well or appropriately behaved. It is the teacher's responsibility to care about the student enough to provide the information needed by the student. This may include a variety of ways of "helping" the student such as repeating directions, devoting extra time, presenting information in multiple ways, and doing anything else that is necessary to make sure the student learns.

As schools have become more inclined to train teachers to act as "facilitators" who simply "guide" students in their "discovery" of concepts, classroom practices have become less and less conducive to learning for African American students who believe the teacher should be an expert who operates with authority. In addition, when schools move toward curricula that do not provide frequent opportunities for structured lessons, African American students and parents can be left wondering when the teacher is going to "teach." As a result, in schools in which teachers are seen as facilitators, African American parents may feel as though the teacher does not care. Students may complain that the teacher is not willing to help the students. This is a basic difference of opinion over the role of teachers.

The most valued teacher, as described by the participants, is the teacher who demonstrates that he/she cares about the students, communicates high expectations to the student along with the parents, communicates a belief that the student can and will achieve, and communicates the purpose of education to the student. It also requires that the teacher maintains a relationship of personal authority, goes the extra mile to help the student learn, repeats things as necessary, and communicates with the student and the parents in a trustworthy and respectful way that displays shared values and comfort with the teacher's role and authority.

For the African American community, the pursuit of education is undertaken for the purpose of obtaining something. It is for the purpose of personal and community uplift and for economic and social empowerment. Knowledge is valued, wisdom is valued, and education is valued. However, formal education has a clear purpose. This has implications for the way that educators interact with young people and the way in which educators communicate with communities. Statements about promoting "lifelong learning" and education "for the sake of education" will seldom resonate with African American parents or students. The value of education stems from what education does for the individual and the community.

In the past, the idea of cultural relevance has been taken to mean that children of color would only want to learn something if it connected to their daily life in the here and now. The true importance of relevance is that students feel as though they are learning for a purpose. When educators speak with young people about the importance of education, these are the values that are more likely to resonate with youth. Students will seldom equate being educated with becoming a better person or obtaining a high status within their own family and community. They are more likely to be motivated by the social, economic, political, and community benefits of education.

African American students need educators to "hang in there" with them. Although children need to be held accountable for their actions, they also must be provided with the opportunity for redemption. A lapse of judgment, responsibility, or commitment that takes place (generally during the preteen and young teen years) should not be used to bar the way for a student's later success. The high expectations of parents and teachers should not be removed. Given the disproportionate suspension and expulsion rate for African American children (particularly boys) and the juvenile incarceration rate, it is critical to ensure that momentary lapses are not allowed to ruin all opportunities available in a young person's life.

Young people must be responsible for their actions and they must be given opportunities to make decisions for their lives. However, when school personnel make decisions about disciplinary actions and responses to academic failure, schools must consider ways to keep doors open for young people so that they will be available at whatever time the young person seeks redemption from their lapse. In elementary and middle schools, short-term lapses in effort and caring should not result in students being removed from rigorous curriculum in which they are exposed to the skills they need to be successful later in life. When educators consider expulsion, it is important to consider at what point a student will be allowed to return to school or, if returning is not an option, what other methods can be used to make the student, parents, and the African American community aware of other options that may be open to the student.

Test scores, suspension, and expulsion rates and other statistics show that the "tween" years (ages 9–12), and the early teen years, up to and including the freshman and sophomore years of high school, are the most dangerous years for African American young people. If schools wish to improve the outcomes for African American children, educators and community members must focus efforts on these years. Educators must ensure that safety nets

Table 5.4.   Do's and Don'ts for Teachers

	Do	Don't
Teachers	• Talk with parents about the structures and expectations within your classroom and school. • Ask parents about their expectations for their children as it relates to school work, grades, and behavior. • Ask parents how they would prefer for you to communicate with them about their children's progress. Communicate often even if this means going out of your way. • Be upfront and honest with parents and students. • Teach parents about the standards their children will be required to meet. • Ask students and parents for input about their needs and seek help for things you do not understand. • Recognize that African American children learn better when they have a meaningful relationship with the teacher. Take time to build the relationship. • Praise high-achieving African American children in the classroom. • Give hard-working African American students (even those with borderline performance) positions of leadership and responsibility. • Personally invite and encourage African American students to take advantage of special opportunities (e.g., honors classes, AP, student leadership, etc.). Provide support for students as needed. • Directly teach students what you expect. Model appropriate behavior, language, etc.	• Keep academic or behavioral concerns to yourself out of fear of the parent's reaction or to help the child avoid punishment. • Assume that African American parents and students view your role as a teacher the same way that you do. • Equate low socioeconomic status with low ability and achievement. • Lower your expectations or overlook or reward inappropriate behavior. • Allow students to "opt out" of learning. • Make predictions or assumptions about your students' futures. • Communicate to students that you do not care about their progress (e.g., "I get paid whether you learn or not.") • Punish students for things they cannot control or judge them based on where they or their parents are in life. • Place African American students in low-level courses or remedial programs that provide no opportunity to reach success.

exist for lapses that do occur and that students can recover from their short-term lapses. Educators must also recognize that for most young people, the "tween" and teen years are the years in which students begin to have power over some of the most important decisions they will make for their future. These years are also probably the worst years for young people to be asked to make these decisions on their own. They need the guidance of both teachers and parents. If education is a transaction between teacher and student with the parent there to monitor the transaction, then these decisions should include both teacher and student and should be closely monitored by a well-informed parent who can share and reinforce his/her expectations for the student.

Schools can close the outcome gap. To do so, educators at all levels must be willing to consider a different view of the educational process. Educators must engage in the educational transaction along with parents and students with the same level of commitment that is typically focused on supporting the educational endowment.

Schools must resist the temptation "help" African American children by treating them just like everyone else. The first thing they must do is begin to gain an understanding of the children being served in schools from the community itself. This study has focused on 15 African American community members. It provides some insight into their discourse on education. Studies like this one are useful in beginning a true dialogue about what is best for African American children in schools. This discussion can never take place without engaging African Americans in the dialogue.

EVERY GOODBYE AIN'T GONE

The purposeful educational transaction is a way to think about the different roles, responsibilities, values, and beliefs shared by African American community members. That said, one of the problems with research is the tendency to overgeneralize results so that information shared simply becomes a different kind of stereotype. Educators, administrators, and policymakers should not use the results of this research to make independent decisions about African American children. Instead, practitioners, researchers, and community members should use this research as the starting point for dialogue, information sharing, and collaboration. Educators and policymakers should work with African American parents, teachers, and community members to consider the impact of their policies, values, and expectations on people who view the educational process differently. Educators cannot help African American children by ignoring the African American community.

The achievement gap cannot be legislated away. Accountability measures, learning standards, testing, school choice, vouchers, and other measures can be beneficial to individual students, schools, and districts, but they cannot eliminate the achievement gap. The outcome gap and the achievement gap ideology must be dismantled as systematically as it has been constructed since the birth of public schools.

As a teenager, it took me a while to figure out what it meant when Daddy would say, "Every closed eye ain't sleep; every goodbye ain't gone." Since then, life has taught me that just because we say goodbye to something, turn away, and stop thinking about it, doesn't mean that it is not everpresent. The outcome gap and the achievement gap ideology linger and fester in our schools and our society. Now, we must go beyond saying goodbye to these problems. We must demonstrate the commitment necessary to usher them out of our schools, communities, and society. The lives of our children depend on it.

References

Anderson, J. 1989. *The education of Blacks in the South: 1860–1935.* Chapel Hill: University of North Carolina.

Apple, M. W. 1990. *Ideology and curriculum.* New York: Routledge.

Asante, M. K. 1998. *The Afrocentric idea.* Revised edition. Philadelphia: Temple University Press.

———. 1990. *The Afrocentric idea.* Updated and revised. Philadelphia: Temple University Press.

———. 1987. *The Afrocentric idea.* Philadelphia: Temple University Press.

Baldwin, J. 1962. *The fire next time.* New York: Vintage.

Bell, D. 1992. *Faces at the bottom of the well: The permanence of racism.* New York: Basic Books.

———. 2004. *Silent covenants: Brown v. Board of Education and the unfulfilled hopes for racial reform.* Oxford: Oxford University Press.

Benson, K. F. 2000. Constructing academic inadequacy: African American athletes' stories of schooling. *Journal of higher education* 71, no. 2, 223–246.

Black boys reject education, on dead-end path, report says. 2007, May 16. *Cleveland Plain Dealer.*

Burnham, S. 1985. *Black intelligence in white society.* New York: Basic Books.

Coleman, J. S. 1966. *Equality of educational opportunity study.* Washington, D.C.: U.S. Department of Health, Education and Welfare.

Conchas, G. Q. 2006. *The color of success: Race and high achieving urban youth.* New York: Teacher's College.

Delpit, L. 1993. *Other peoples' children: Cultural conflict in the classroom.* New York: New Press.

Diamond, J. B. & Gomez, K. 2004. African American parents' educational orientations: The importance of social class and parents' perceptions of schools. *Education and urban society* 36, no. 4, 383–427.

Dillard, C. B. 2000. The substance of things hoped for, the evidence of things not seen: Examining an endarkened feminist epistemology in educational research and leadership. *Qualitative studies in education* 13, no. 6, 661–681.

Douglass, F. 1845. *Narrative of the life of Frederick Douglass, an American slave.* Boston: American Anti-Slavery Society.

———. 2000 [1865]. What the black man wants. In *Let nobody turn us around: Voices of resistance, reform, and renewal.* Lanham, MD: Rowman & Littlefield.

Du Bois, W. E. B. 1903. *The souls of black folk.* New York: Penguin.

———. 1904. Edited by Lewis, D. L. (1995). *W. E. B. Du Bois: A reader.* New York: Henry Holt.

———. 1935. Does the Negro need separate schools? *The journal of Negro education* 4, no. 3, 328–335.

Ford, M. D. 1991, July 24. Defending the common school. *The Nation.*

Genesis 8:25. *The Holy Bible*, King James Version.

Gitlin, A. 1994. *Power and method: Political activism and educational research.* New York: Routledge.

Gould, S. J. 1981. *The mismeasure of man.* New York: W. W. Norton.

Graves, J. L. 2005. *The race myth: Why we pretend race exists in America.* New York: Penguin.

Hale, J. 2001. *Learning while black: Creating educational excellence for African American children.* Baltimore: Johns Hopkins University.

Hallinan, M. T. 2001. Sociological perspectives on black-white inequalities in American schooling. *Sociology of education.* 50–70.

Hebert, T. P. 1998. Gifted black males in an urban high school: Factors that influence achievement and underachievement. *Journal for the education of the gifted* 21, no. 4, 385–414.

Herrnstein, R. J. & Murray, C. 1994. The bell curve: Intelligence and class structure in American life. New York: Free Press.

Honora, D. 2003. Urban African American adolescents and school identification. *Urban education* 38, no. 1, 58–76.

hooks, b. 1997. Representing whiteness in the black imagination. In *Displacing whiteness: Essays in social & cultural criticism.* Durham, NC: Duke University Press.

Howard, T. C. 2002. Hearing footsteps in the dark: African American students' descriptions of effective teachers. *Journal of education for students placed at risk* 7, no. 4, 425–444.

———. 2003. "A tug of war for our minds": African American high school students' perceptions of their academic identities and college aspirations. *High school journal* 87, no. 1, 4–17.

Hubbard, L. 1999. College aspirations among low-income African American high school students: Gendered strategies for success. *Anthropology & education quarterly* 30, no. 3, 363–383.

Hwang, Y. S., Echols, C. & Vrongistinos, K. 2002. Multidimensional academic motivation of high achieving African American students. *College student journal* 36, no. 4, 544–554.

Jefferson, T. 1787. *Notes on the state of Virginia. In The negro versus equality.* Chicago: Rand McNally.

Jencks, C. 1972. *Inequality: A reassessment of the effect of family and schooling in America.* New York: Basic Books.

Jensen, A. M. 1973. *Educability and group differences.* New York: Harper and Row.

Jordan, W. D. 1969. *The negro versus equality: 1762—826.* Chicago: Rand McNally.

Jordan, W. J. & Cooper, R. 2003. High school reform and black male students: Limits and possibilities of policy and practice. *Urban education* 38, no. 2, 196–216.

Kaplan, E. B. 1999. "It's going good": Inner-city black and latino adolescents' perceptions about achieving in education. *Urban education* 34, no. 2, 181–213.

Katz, W. L. 1967. *Eyewitness: The negro in American history.* New York: Pitman.

King, J. E. 2005. *Black education: A transformative research and action agenda for the new century.* Washington, D.C.: American Educational Research Association.

Krueger, R. A. 1994. *Focus groups: A practical guide for applied research.* Thousand Oaks, CA: Sage Publications.

Kvale, S. 1996. *InterViews: An introduction to qualitative research interviewing.* London: Sage.

Ladson-Billings, G. 1994. *The dreamkeepers: Successful teachers of African American students.* New York: Jossey-Bass.

———. 2006. From the achievement gap to the education debt: Understanding achievement in U.S. schools. *Educational researcher* 35, no. 7, 3–12.

Long, E. 2002 [1788]. *The history of Jamaica, or general survey of the ancient and modern state of that Island.* Montreal: McGill-Queens University Press.

Marable, M. & Mulling, L. eds. 2000. *Let nobody turn us around: Voices of resistance, reform and renewal.* New York: Rowman & Littlefield.

Marshall, T. 1954. The Brown decision and the struggle for school desegregation. In *Let nobody turn us around: Voices of resistance, reform and renewal.* New York: Rowman & Littlefield.

Meier, A. 1963. *Negro thought in America, 1880–1915: Racial ideologies in the age of Booker T. Washington.* Ann Arbor: University of Michigan.

Milam, J. H. 1992. The emerging paradigm of afrocentric research methods. Paper presented at Annual Meeting of the Association for the Study of Higher Education. Minneapolis, MN: ASHE.

Miller, L. P. 1974. *The testing of black students.* Englewood Cliffs, NJ: Prentice-Hall.

Moynihan, D. P. 1965. *The negro family: The case for national action.* Washington, D.C.: U.S. Department of Labor.

Noguera, P. A. 2003. The trouble with black boys: The role and influence of environmental and cultural factors on the academic performance of African American males. *Urban education* 38, no. 4, 431–459.

Ogbu, J. U. 1978. *Minority education and caste: The American system in cross-cultural perspective.* New York: Academic Press.

———. 2003. *Black American students in an affluent suburb: A study of academic disengagement.* New York: Lawrence Erlbaum.

Ogbu, J. U. & Fordham, S. 1986. Black students' school success: Coping with the burden of "acting white." *Urban review* 18, no. 3, 176–206.

Parents Involved with Community Schools v. Seattle School District No. 1, 551 U.S. 2007.

Perry, T., Steele, C. & Hilliard III, A. 2003. *Young, gifted and black: Promoting high achievement among African American students.* Boston: Beacon Press.

Pino, N. W. & Smith, W. L. 2004. African American students, the academic ethic and GPA. *Journal of Black Studies* 35, no. 1, 113–131.

Sanders, M. G. 1997. Overcoming obstacles: Academic achievement as a response to racism and discrimination. *Journal of negro education* 66, no. 1, 83–93.

Scheurich, J. J. & Young, M. D. 1997. Coloring epistemologies: Are our research epistemologies racially biased? *Educational researcher* 26, no. 4, 4–15.

Schools slow in closing gaps between races. 2007, June 1. *New York Times.*

Schwitzer, A. M., Griffin, O. T., Ancis, J. R. & Thomas, C. R. 1999. Social adjustment experiences of African American college students. *Journal of counseling & development* 77, no. 2, 189–197.

Seidman, I. E. 1991. *Interviewing as qualitative research: A guide for researchers in education and the social sciences.* New York: Teachers College.

Sewell, W. H. and Hauser, R. M. 1975. *Education, occupation and earnings: Achievement in the early career.* New York: Academic Press.

Siddle Walker, V. 2001. African American teaching in the South: 1940–1960. *American educational research journal* 38, no. 4, 751–779.

Singham, M. 2003. *The achievement gap in U.S. education: Canaries in the mine.* New York: Rowman & Littlefield Education.

Success rate still lags for blacks who take AP tests. 2007, June 29. *The Washington Post.*

Tillman, L. C. 2002. Culturally sensitive research approaches: An African-American perspective. *Educational Researcher* 31, no. 9, 3–12.

———. 2006. Researching and writing from an African-American perspective: Reflective notes on three research studies. *International journal of qualitative studies in education* 19, no. 3, 265–287.

Tuzon, S. and Violas, P. 1993. *School and society.* New York: McGraw-Hill.

Vaughn, S., Schumm J. S. & Sinagub, J. 1996. *Focus group interviews in education and psychology.* London: Sage.

Washington, B. T. 1901. *Up from slavery.* New York: Doubleday.

Wasonga, T. & Christman, D. E. 2003. Perceptions and construction of meaning of urban high school experiences among African American university students: A focus group approach. *Education and urban society* 35, no. 2, 181–201.

Watkins, W. H. 2001. *The white architects of black education: Ideology and power in America, 1865–1954.* New York: Teachers College Press.

Webster's New Collegiate Dictionary. 1986. New York: G & C Merriam.

Wells, A. S. and Crain, R. 1997. *Stepping over the color line: African-American student in white suburban schools.* New Haven, CT: Yale University Press.

West, Cornell, interview by Tavis Smiley, *Tavis Smiley Late Night on PBS*, PBS, September 2007.

Woodsen, C. G. 1922. *The negro in our history.* Washington D.C.: Associated Publishers.

———. 1933. *The mis-education of the negro.* Trenton, NJ: Associated Press.

About the Author

In her work as an educator and consultant, **Teresa D. Hill** works to make the system work for every child. Her motto is "All children can learn . . . period."

Dr. Hill received her bachelor's degree in elementary education, and her master and doctor of education degrees in educational administration from Illinois State University where she researched the "achievement gap." She began her career teaching a kindergarten class of thirty-one students from low income backgrounds and later served as an assistant principal, principal, and assistant superintendent. Dr. Hill consults with educational leaders, provides professional development for teachers, and leads school improvement planning. She lives in Illinois with her husband Bishop A. Q. Hill and their son, David.